"I loved this book! *Destiny Thieves* got my attention from beginning to end. Sandie Freed has a unique way of addressing the major issues and *-ites* that we will face if our expected end is to be greater than our beginning. Sandie gives practical steps to end compromise, discouragement and a weakened soulish constitution so we can walk in victory in a changing world. She has learned to submit herself to God and resist the enemies that would stop her from walking in joy and with authority. *Destiny Thieves* is a 'treasury of swords' for any prayer warrior who wants to conquer his or her enemy! As the spiritual war intensifies in the days ahead, this is one book that will keep you sharpened and on the offensive in battle."

Chuck D. Pierce, president, Glory of Zion International;
vice president, Global Harvest Ministries

"*Destiny Thieves* is a must-read for every church leader and saint in the Body of Christ. Sandie's insight on the demonic spirits assigned to cut off the individual destinies of people as well as the corporate destiny of the Church is powerful. These are remarkable times for those who are pressing in to fulfill their divine calling. This book will be used as a weapon in the arsenal as believers do battle to fulfill their highest call."

Jane Hamon, apostle and co-pastor,
Christian International Family Church

"Life is full of challenges. Many of them are a result of a spiritual war unseen by the physical eye. To overcome and break through, it is essential to see behind the scenes of problems, obstacles and hindrances. Here is a great book, written from practical experience, that discusses how to identify the enemy and then what to do about it. Sandie knows what she is talking about. Read it and you will learn how to overcome and break through."

Barbara Yoder, senior pastor, Shekinah Christian Church; Michigan state coordinator, United States Strategic Prayer Network; founder, Breakthrough Apostolic Ministries Network

"Sandie did not receive these divine insights simply by reading books. She received them from being on the front line of ministry, from her personal experiences in dealing with people and from discovering supernaturally the 'destiny thieves' that are sent from hell to stop Christians from fulfilling their calling in Christ Jesus.

"Thanks, Sandie, for allowing God to take you through the challenging processes to bring forth these vital truths to the people of God everywhere."

from the foreword by **Dr. Bill Hamon**, chairman, founder and bishop, Christian International Ministries Network

"*Destiny Thieves* does exactly what the subtitle promises—it exposes seducing spirits. Few contemporary writers offer the insight and understanding Sandie Freed shares in her timely and informative work. Using the spiritual perception of a prophet and personal experience gained during her years of pastoral ministry, she pulls aside the cloak of darkness behind which the enemy has hidden to deceive. Though the subject is frightful in its scope, we are made to understand that we have a destiny to fulfill and that our Father God is committed to us and to our success. The best-laid plans of darkness will not prevent what Jesus intends for His disciples—if we do not remain ignorant of Satan's devices. *Destiny Thieves* lifts the veil."

Dr. Jim Davis, president, Christian International Apostolic Network

Destiny Thieves

Defeat Seducing Spirits and Achieve Your Purpose in God

Sandie Freed

Chosen
Grand Rapids, Michigan

Published by Chosen Books
a division of Baker Publishing Group
P.O. Box 6287, Grand Rapids, MI 49516-6287
www.chosenbooks.com

Printed in the United States of America

                    Library of Congress Cataloging-in-Publication Data
Freed, Sandie, 1951–
    Destiny thieves : defeat seducing spirits and achieve your purpose in
  God / Sandie Freed.
       p.   cm.
    Includes bibliographical references.
    ISBN 10: 0-8007-9420-6 (pbk.)
    ISBN 978-0-8007-9420-0 (pbk.)
    1. Spiritual warfare. I. Title.
  BV4509.5.F747 2007
  235'.4—dc22   2006024913

Unless otherwise indicated, Scripture is taken from the King James Version of
the Bible.

Scripture marked NASB is taken from the New American Standard Bible®, Copy-
right © 1960, 1962, 1963, 1968, 1971, 1972, 1973, 1975, 1977, 1995 by The Lockman
Foundation. Used by permission.

Scripture marked NLT is taken from the Holy Bible, New Living Translation, copy-
right © 1996. Used by permission of Tyndale House Publishers, Inc., Wheaton,
Illinois 60189. All rights reserved.

09   10   11   12   13   14   15   9   8   7   6   5   4   3

To my husband, Mickey,
who labors with me to fulfill destiny
and never allows me to "settle" for less
than my potential.

To my daughter, Kim Freed Putman,
who is still the "best thing I ever did,"
and her husband, Matt,
for their support and love even when I am unlovable.

To my mother, Dena Davis,
who is the most courageous
and determined woman I know
and who has always pressed me to be the same.

To my father, Bud Davis,
who is fulfilling his eternal destiny in heaven.

Finally, to my Lord Jesus Christ,
who fulfilled His destiny
to empower me to fulfill mine.

Contents

Acknowledgments

Writing a book takes a commitment from an author, but the author is not alone in fulfilling its completion. Multitudes of people are involved in this type of project, including intercessors who pray, families who sacrifice time and those who stand alongside supporting the vision.

I would like to acknowledge specifically four very precious friends who have stayed awake into the late night hours editing and proofreading. They also have served as my personal intercessors and have prayed me through the completion of this mission. Sarah Amanor, Paula Bledsoe, Vicki Caldwell and Kathy Shaw, thank you for your support and prayers. I love you guys! We did it!

I thank my sister, Pam Garris, and her husband, David. This powerful team labored with us for many years and continues to serve as leaders within Zion Ministries. Pam and David, thank you for continuing to carry the torch!

To all the ordained and licensed ministers of Zion Ministries, your support has been an underlying strength to me. During times of transition, your faithfulness has been a sustaining force of encouragement.

I acknowledge apostles Jim and Jeanni Davis, apostolic oversight for Christian International Apostolic Network.

I honor and respect you more each year I serve and labor with you. You have been examples of faith and perseverance. Thank you for your godly example and covenant relationship.

To apostles Tom and Jane Hamon: Over the years you were very instrumental in providing needed support and courage as I gained revelation for this book. Thank you for sharing your wisdom and insight concerning spiritual strongholds and discernment. Observing your dedication to the Lord has inspired me to believe for God's very best.

I also acknowledge apostle Leon Walters. You have served on the board of Zion Ministries for more than a decade and labored faithfully with us through the good times as well as the bad times. Mickey and I highly esteem you and thank you for being a mentor as well as a special friend.

To my spiritual parents, Bishop Bill and Mom Evelyn Hamon: Thank you for continuing to believe in me and for challenging me with new opportunities for growth and maturity. I honor you for your determination and commitment to fulfill all God has for you, and especially for never giving up on me or my destiny.

For the endless editing and typesetting I have depended upon Tim Cole. He has remained encouraging as well as patient with all the rushed, last-minute retypes. Thank you!

And I thank the staff, members and leaders of Faith Christian Center, who served the Lord with us during the years that we were pastors (1990–2004). This book is the culmination of fourteen years of research and study. Your support through the years made it possible for me to find strength as I pressed for the revelation needed for this book. We worshiped together, labored together and fulfilled destiny together. God bless each of you as you continue moving forward into your divine fulfillment.

Foreword

We who believe God created humankind for a divine purpose believe Adam and Eve were created with a destiny to fulfill: filling the earth with humankind in God's own image and likeness. But before Adam and Eve were created, one of God's angelic beings rebelled against God and was cast out of heaven to become an opposer of all God destines to happen. This being became known as Satan, the devil, prince of darkness, etc. Satan seduced one-third of the angels into joining him. When they were cast out of heaven to earth they became evil, seducing spirits. Adam and Eve were seduced by Satan, causing them to fail to fulfill their destiny. Then Jesus came and provided redemption for humankind to become a new creation with the destiny to be in God's image and likeness. Those who have accepted Jesus Christ as Savior and Lord have divine destinies to fulfill. Satan, however, has a host of "destiny thieves" who have been commissioned by Satan to stop God's people from fulfilling their divine destinies on earth.

Sandie Freed has unveiled the manipulative, deceitful and seductive tactics used by Satan to prevent, hinder and stop God's people from fulfilling their destinies. Her book will be a liberating force. It will set captives free and equip the saints with revelation knowledge and spiritual truth that will enable them to avoid the traps of the enemy and to overcome when tempted. Knowing truth enables one to fulfill destiny.

The truths and divine insights revealed in this book should be known by every saint, especially those in leadership positions. As you read each chapter you will think, *This is great, helpful and so enlightening.* When you begin to think there could not be much more truth on this matter, read on. The next chapter will be even more enlightening and enabling.

One of the hidden blessings is the realization that people's destinies are as diverse as the different members of the human body. Some are called to build great works for God such as megachurches and worldwide organizations. Others are called to go through certain processes, experiences and ministries that cause them to discover great truths that bless humankind. This is what Sandie is doing by writing this book.

Sandie and Mickey Freed have experienced many things that have resulted in revelation knowledge that will enable millions of Christians to fulfill their destinies. Sandie did not receive these divine insights simply by reading books. She received them from being on the front line of ministry, from her personal experiences in dealing with people and from discovering supernaturally the "destiny thieves" that are sent from hell to stop Christians from fulfilling their calling in Christ Jesus.

Thanks, Sandie, for allowing God to take you through the challenging processes to bring forth these vital truths to the people of God everywhere. This book is destined to be a vital tool for enabling Christians to fulfill their calling and destinies.

Dr. Bill Hamon
Chairman, Founder and Bishop of Christian
International Ministries Network;
Founder of Christian International Apostolic Network

Dr. Hamon is author of seven major books:

The Eternal Church

Prophets and Personal Prophecy

Prophets and the Prophetic Movement

Prophets, Pitfalls and Principles

Apostles, Prophets and the Coming Moves of God

The Day of the Saints

Who Am I and Why Am I Here?

Introduction

I Want to Live and Fulfill Destiny!

Destiny—something to which a person or thing is destined; a predetermined course of events.[1]

O Lord, please let this be a good report! It was such a desperate plea that I began to beg. *Please, Lord. I have stood on Your Word. I have done all I know to do. I do not want to die!* These words silently repeated themselves as I dialed my physician's office for the latest results of my blood tests.

Anyone who has been forced to wait for laboratory reports can identify with the tormenting fear that occurred during the delays. It is especially severe when you sense the spirit of death lurking at the door just waiting for the opportunity to seize your hope and life.

The secretary placed me on hold. More anxiety flooded my thoughts. My heart beat rapidly, a cold sweat formed upon my brow and my legs felt as if they were literally buckling beneath me.

I prepared myself as I waited for the nurse to return to the phone.

If I receive another bad report, how will I respond this time?

Up to this point I had found the strength to move forward. Somehow I had been empowered to dig down deep within my spirit to find enough faith to believe God would come through for me.

Would it be different this time? I felt I had come to the end of my rope.

God, I absolutely cannot find renewed strength to go on!

I soon found myself running to the bedroom, sobbing. I threw myself across the bed. Another negative report had shaken me to the core. The latest "death sentence" poisoned my thoughts and emotions. I had little hope left, I concluded.

"Will this battle against this destructive viral infection ever end?" I screamed aloud while pleading for my life.

"I can't take this anymore, God! I just can't take it! I am going to die, and I have not fulfilled my destiny!"

I now realize that I did not fully understand the meaning of *destiny*. All I understood at the time was that I felt extremely void and desperate for life. I wanted to do so much for the Lord but did not understand how it could ever manifest. I now understand that everyone endures a process of preparation while fulfilling destiny and that God has desired results for each of us that complete His planned destiny.

For me, it was a long battle continuing to choose life. At the time, I did not possess the revelation that what I was experiencing was part of the process in "the making of a minister." Every mountain of tribulation, every test, every wilderness experience was the needed preparation for the possessing of my Promised Land. While enduring each storm, it became increasingly difficult to find the light through the dark clouds. Through every tunnel of darkness I traveled, I was forced to trust the Lord and find strength in His ability to sustain and guide me.

Hindsight is 20/20, and looking back I fully understand that the Lord desired to become my compass. It was as if I were a ship captain being trained to follow a spiritual compass while I sailed through rough seas during stormy conditions. The training I was receiving was not to focus on the storm but to focus on His Word and His report in every situation. I was involved in boot camp training, learning to exercise levels of greater faith. This was all necessary for a future destiny that He had planned for my life.

But this particular storm felt like a hurricane! The winds were so fierce my ship was being tossed back and forth. I felt as if I were thrown to the edge and about to be flung overboard. I did not know if I could persevere because there seemed to be no strength left to fight. I felt as if I could not hold on any longer.

In the natural, death appeared to be imminent. There seemed to be nothing I could do about this situation, and I found myself totally out of control. My situation seemed hopeless. "There is nothing else I can do except lie down and die," I continued to cry out, begging God to help me.

"Lord," I said His name between sobs, "if You will let me live, I promise to serve You. If You will extend my life, I will serve You with every fiber of my being. For the rest of my entire life I will do whatever You want me to do!

"Lord, I have not yet begun to fulfill my destiny. I have not done enough to serve You. Please let me fulfill Your plans for my life."

Suddenly I felt impressed to read Jeremiah 29:11: "For I know the thoughts that I think towards you, saith the LORD, thoughts of peace, and not of evil, to give you an expected end." I meditated on this passage. *What is an expected end?* I curiously sought out *Strong's Concordance*. Was the Lord actually telling me that He would heal me? Did He really have a destiny for me to fulfill? Did He have plans for me that I did not know?

I later realized that the answer to all my questions was yes! God did have a plan for my life. God did plan for me to fulfill destiny. He had an "expected end" of fulfillment for me.

The "Expected End"

The phrase *expected end* actually means "an expectation and ground of hope." It also implies that we are "to lie in wait for" (hope) and also translates "to bind together" (as if we are to bind our hope and expectations together to achieve an expected end).[2]

How exciting to realize that God desired to give me *ground* to hope—a foundation of hope upon which I needed to build with words of faith. This word from God was fertile soil. As I would continue to plant His promises into that soil of divine hope, then I surely would achieve my destiny. From that point I was able to bind every promise together and expect my miracle. For the first time since I developed the viral infection, I was able to believe! Expectation and hope were firmly stabilized within my spirit. Now every promise God gave me was sown into the ground of hope and expectation.

But the miracle did not come quickly. I labored for my healing, struggling to come out of my wilderness of death and infirmity. Many fears and mind-sets were roadblocks I had to break through. The barriers of uncertainties were similar to computer chips of negativity, which were deeply imbedded in my mind. The grim outlook seemed impossible to dislodge. I was convinced that I was destined to die prematurely; after all, the doctors said I would die. Tormented during the nights with disturbing dreams of death, I was bombarded with discouragement, confusion and exhaustion. I struggled to trust the Lord and believe in faith that I would be healed, but my faith eventually gave way to the spirit of death and each day seemed to be filled with tormenting thoughts of funeral services.

Then a phone call came that changed my life.

"Sandie, you have got to go with me to Christian International and let the prophets minister life to you!" It was my friend on the phone. She had been praying for my recovery for months on end.

"Go where? What is Christian International?"

"Well," she began to inform me, "it is an organization founded by Dr. Bill Hamon. He has gathered a company of prophets that know how to hear from God. I believe you need to go and ask the prophets to minister life to you. I just know they are a key to releasing your destiny!"

My exposure to the prophetic ministry was limited, but I did understand the power of the prophetic word. Years earlier a prophet had ministered a personal word to me. The prophetic word and insight were so accurate and the anointing so tangible that there was no doubt God was in the midst.

Could this be the time of my breakthrough? Could this be my opportunity to be released into destiny? "When can we go?" I jumped at the chance for life!

Within a few weeks we were on an airplane headed for Florida to attend a Christian International prophetic conference, an event that radically changed my life. Attending that conference gave me fresh insight into fulfilling my destiny. Prophets Dr. Mary Crum and Dr. Leon Walters (both ordained ministers with Christian International) ministered that God had a destiny for me to fulfill, that God was not finished with me yet! Their words, "You shall live and not die and proclaim the word of the Lord," still resound through my spirit as I remember the first time they ministered to me.

When I received these words, I leaped from my chair and began to shout for joy! Suddenly the revelation of Jeremiah 29:11 became reality and a revelation. It was at that time I realized that God DID have a plan for me and that He planned healing and restoration for my life. God had "good thoughts" and not "evil thoughts" toward me, and He had expectations for me to fulfill. He had an expected end!

It was only a few days later that I heard Bishop Bill Hamon, who later became my spiritual father, minister on the spirit of Caleb, the Old Testament example of courage, determination, faith and vision to possess his mountain and enter into the destiny God had planned for him. Numbers 14:24 states, "But my servant Caleb, because he had another spirit with him, and hath followed me fully, him will I bring into the land whereinto he went; and his seed shall possess it." Caleb had another spirit, and this made him different from the other twelve spies who surveyed Canaan. Caleb was different in the fact that he followed God to the fullest. God had a predetermined, planned destiny of possession for Caleb and for Caleb's generations. But also there would be warfare; Caleb would have to fight for the possession of his mountain: "(Now the Amalekites and the Canaanites dwelt in the valley.) Tomorrow turn you, and get you into the wilderness by the way of the Red sea" (Numbers 14:25). Caleb's destiny involved first defeating the Canaanites and the Amalekites.

These two ancient enemies of Israel have much to teach us today, as they are representative of the spiritual enemies we battle for our destinies. In order to fully inherit my destiny, I needed to be like Caleb. I needed to rise up with great courage, move forward and defeat the "ites" of Canaan, especially the Amalekite stronghold that blocked my destiny.

Caleb overcame the wilderness, doubt and unbelief and gained possession of his promised mountain. Caleb's positive report "Give me my mountain!" began to take root in my heart. *Lord, I have a destiny, and I will fulfill it!* Finally, hope had been planted firmly in my ground. I now believed, beyond any doubt, that my destiny could be fulfilled.

Becoming Determined for Destiny

This was my new beginning. My life was totally transformed due to the prophetic insight I received. I had a destiny, and I became *determined for destiny.* I know in my heart that it was time to set my face like flint toward my future and desired end.

Being determined means being "staunch and unwavering." It also means that we are to decide, implying that we must make a decision and then not waver in that decision.[3] In order for me to move forward in conquest, I finally had to decide that I wanted whatever God had for my future and then lock into hope and faith, not wavering.

Possession is a three-step process. First, one must make a firm decision to move forward. Second, one must set one's face like flint toward destiny. I did both of these after attending the conference that changed my life. The third step, however, is where the real work begins. It is walking in the empowerment of His grace to move forward and possess one's mountain of inheritance.

It was a two-year battle with the spirit of death before I was completely healed from the viral infection. For two years my husband and I warred with my prophetic word before I experienced the faithfulness of His promise. We were faithful, as Paul instructed Timothy, to "war a good warfare" over my prophecies for breakthrough (see 1 Timothy 1:18). Many hours were spent playing our taped prophetic words, pacing the floor together and declaring God's Word over my body.

Then came the time when I heard the doctors say these glorious words, "Sandie, there are no test results reporting any more infection!"

Yes, finally, I was beginning to fulfill destiny—the beginning of the plans and expected end of which God speaks. My mountain of death dissolved, just as the Lord had promised. I am now an ordained prophetess of the Lord receiving the spiritual oversight of Dr. Bill Hamon. My husband and I served as pastors of Faith Christian Center in Bedford, Texas, for fourteen years and now have established Zion Ministries Apostolic/Prophetic Training Center in the same area. We travel extensively, representing Christian International Apostolic Network. Together as an apostolic-prophetic team we are fulfilling the Ephesians 4:11 commission of the five-fold ministry, training and equipping the saints to do the work of the ministry.

When I look over my shoulder into the past and observe how far the grace of God has brought me, often I am overwhelmed. I had felt as if I were a nothing going nowhere! I had viewed myself as sick, weak and mentally incapable. But God saw me as healed, strong and being used for His Kingdom. He had so many wonderful plans for my life! To consider that He could desire to use me to train others in the prophetic ministry, dreams and visions, counseling, intercession, miracles and other areas of spiritual gifting is amazing to me. I have been going somewhere—in Him— ever since I grabbed hold of destiny.

You Have a Destiny

Did you know that you also have a destiny? That you also have an "expected end" that God has planned? Do you have mountains in your life that seem insurmountable? Did you know that you also can possess the courage, strength and determination of Caleb to possess your mountain? Maybe you are in a situation similar to mine. Maybe you have experienced hopeless situations and you feel as if you are not fulfilling your potential. Maybe you are desperate for answers to your situations.

You may not have experienced the life-altering change I encountered through the prophetic ministry of a prophet, but understand this: The Bible is full of prophetic words! Yes, the Bible speaks the Word of God and His desire for good things in your life. His plans for you are just as they are for me—good and not evil! All through the Word of God are prophecies of life, healing, restoration and fulfillment.

There Is an Enemy

But also realize this: There is an enemy, the prince of this world who has a plan of destruction. The devil, our adversary, comes to steal, kill and destroy (see John 10:10). He is a thief, and he desires to steal your destiny. He has many different tactics to snatch you out from the plans of God. There are quite possibly strongholds in your land of promise. The Amalekites, a tribe who robs destiny, are probably in your territory and must be driven out in order for you to possess your promise.

Esther had the favor of the Lord and was born for such a time. But she also had an enemy, Haman the Agagite (a descendant of the Amalekites), who plotted to destroy her, her family and her entire race! Each of us is an Esther. The devil does not desire simply to destroy us; he wants our entire families, businesses, churches and nations. And he will not stop there—I have said many times that if you ask the devil to dinner, he will bring his entire suitcase. He has plans to remain if we open any door and allow entrance.

If you have ever vowed to serve God, the devil will come to steal your confession. I vowed that if He would heal me, I would be obedient to serve Him and do whatever He asked. My vows were tested many times, but God gave me the grace to achieve victory.

23

Throughout the years the Lord has revealed many different strongholds that destroy the seeds of destiny. This book exposes the different satanic strategies that rob God's children of potential—the destiny thieves that rob your future. But the following chapters also present many divine strategies to empower your faith and achieve victory and the destiny that has been created for you. It is time to unmask and expose the secret strategies of seduction by the destiny thieves!

We are at war. We are God's army. Yes, this will be a battle—but a battle very worthwhile! Remember: There is no great victory without a battle!

Onward, Christian Soldiers!

Father, You are in control of our destinies. You are the Alpha and the Omega, the Beginning and the End. Your Word says that You have plans for each of us and You have good thoughts toward us. Lord, we thank You for every good thought and every good plan that You have ordained for us. You are the Author and Finisher of our faith. Thank You for imparting a new measure of faith within us. We choose life, and we choose to believe that You have a destiny for each of us to fulfill. Thank You for empowering us to fulfill Your plans in us and for us. This day we choose to set our faces like flint. We choose to be obedient vessels, observing Your Word and being faithful to walk in the direction You have chosen for us. We choose to be like Caleb, to be people of a different spirit to fully follow after Your future plans for us. We are determined to serve You. We declare that our household will continue to serve You all the days of our lives! Now, Lord, open our hearts and minds to new revelation so that we may fully embrace whatever steps are needed to fulfill our destinies and take our mountains!

Amen.

Important Definitions to Consider

thief—someone who *steals*, especially *secretly*[4]

steal—to take without permission or right, especially *secretly* or by force[5]

secret—something *hidden* from sight, without general knowledge[6]

exposure—an act of revealing or unmasking[7]

seduction—the act of being seduced, led astray from duty or principles; corrupt, attract, win over and entice[8]

One

Destiny Thieves

The thief cometh not, but for to steal, and to kill, and to destroy: I am come that they might have life, and that they might have it more abundantly.

John 10:10

The sun was beaming through the windshield, just short of a glare, as I drove to church on that lovely Sunday morning in spring. My expectations were rising up within my spirit, believing God for a divine visitation. I was so full of faith that it seemed I could almost reach out and touch God's glory. I turned up the volume of my favorite cassette and tried desperately to outsing the singers on the tape, "jiving and nodding" as I lifted my voice to the Lord.

Nothing can steal my joy today! I thought to myself. *This is the day the Lord has made, and I will rejoice and be glad in it!*

My fingers tapped against the steering wheel, keeping beat with the drum sounds echoing through the speakers. I felt like a teenager moving my entire body along with the music. Why, I could even rap to this! I was totally boasting in my good day.

I wheeled into the parking lot of our church where we had been pastoring for more than a decade. The crepe myrtles were blooming in fragrance; the flowerbeds were birthing the fruits of planted seeds.

The grounds are well manicured and beautiful. It is a wonderful day!

I acknowledged a familiar face and waved as I found my designated parking place. I glanced at another vehicle entering the parking lot and waved again, still smiling and joyful.

I made my way into the building, humming to the music that was still playing in my head. As I advanced toward the office I was met by a member of our pastoral team. I greeted him with a smile, yet noticed the unreturned gesture. It did not take a rocket scientist to discern from his expression that something would attempt to destroy my good day.

My heart sank. *Not more bad news!* I silently groaned as my emotions ran amuck. *O Lord, this is too beautiful a day to have it spoiled. When will this ever end?*

I sat down to prepare myself for another negative report concerning our congregation. I thought the battle was over and that we were experiencing breakthrough. The devil, however, was still at work.

The Accuser of the Brethren

And I heard a loud voice saying in heaven, Now is come salvation, and strength, and the kingdom of our God, and the power of his Christ: for the *accuser of our brethren* is cast down, which accused them before our God day and night.

Revelation 12:10 (emphasis mine)

Six months earlier we had been tempted to resign as pastors, to basically throw in the towel—actually, not just one towel but every towel we had ever owned and used in any capacity. Now, after standing for such a lengthy season and finally experiencing a breakthrough, we were finding ourselves back in battle against more of the enemy's plans of destruction.

My husband and I had been senior pastors for years. Our ability to survive and remain in the Christian race consisted of continual recommitments and renewed decisions to "lock back in" to fulfill destiny. The battle with the accuser of the brethren had been relentless. It seemed as if we could barely catch our breath from a previous onslaught before another "air raid" targeted us. At times I even imagined myself enlisted in the Air Force during World War II, flying a dive-bomber while dodging bullets from the enemy.

Leaving Our Post

The care pastor followed me to my office, and I prepared my heart, emotions and mind to hear the results of another evil assignment. Once again I bowed my head as I was informed that one of our leaders had forsaken the "call" and had chosen to leave the ministry and backslide into an old lifestyle. His wife and he had returned to their spiritual Egypt, deciding it was too difficult to live for the Lord. The leader had left his post, forsaken his anointing and retreated into a "comfortable" place. My heart sank in despair.

He was so gifted, I silently told the Lord. *We needed him. We had so many plans to use him in ministry.* I was sad that we lost him because he was special to us. We had known him for years, mentored him and observed his spiritual growth toward maturity. And I became even more discouraged to lose another quality leader to "comfort zones." Actually I was being somewhat selfish; my husband and I desperately needed dedicated and proven servants, and here we were, losing one of proven quality.

After the conversation, I closed my office door. Immediately tears filled my eyes and found their way down my face. Once again, I began crying out loud, begging God for an answer.

"Why, God, why? What is happening to our leaders? They are constantly being attacked, and they quit. Just when they are on the verge of breakthrough, they give up!" I poured out my concerns to the Lord.

The Thief

The Lord answered with an astounding vision. I saw a strong seducing spirit, in the form of a thief. This thief was successfully stealing God's leaders, seductively drawing them away from their position and inheritance.

First, he would seduce them into believing the lie that they did not belong, that they did not "fit" any longer. As a result, each of them would separate from the church body. Once he had them alone, unprotected and vulnerable, he would strip them of their power and authority, stealing their destiny. Before the enemy convinced them to exit, we would notice complaints such as, "I can't find my place in the body," "I don't seem to have a place anymore," "No one cares about me in this church," and "No one calls me anymore. I need a church that cares."

Even though we made many attempts to contact the sheep and tried every possible way to prove our love and concern, it was never enough. They had already been separated in their hearts.

Jezebel

The seducing spirit in the vision was in the form of a type of Jezebel—the "painted lady" in the Scriptures who dressed seductively, murdered the prophets and threatened to destroy Elijah (see 1 Kings 18–19; 2 Kings 9:30). This idolatrous queen also worked in unity with the sons of Belial, falsely accusing Naboth, stealing from and then murdering him (see 1 Kings 21).

Although it had no gender, I knew in my spirit that the thief represented Jezebel. In the vision her countenance changed from a seductive-type person into a thief or bandit-type character. Once more, the countenance transformed into a person plagued with uncleanness and defilement—revealing that this seducing spirit was also a perverted, unclean spirit. (Jezebel and the unclean spirit are further explained in chapters 11 and 12.)

Our church was not experiencing an isolated attack; this was the enemy's strategy against every area of ministry within God's Church, which made its impact in the spirit-realm. In the vision it was clear that the result of this demonically inspired attack was the seduction and apostasy of godly leaders and saints. The spirit of deception was so overpowering that it was deceiving God's elect!

Then I heard the Lord speak concerning the sheep and the precious servants that He had appointed to support us. The vision continued to unfold, and the Lord revealed a demonic assignment to steal the anointing and destiny from His chosen ones. Saints who had tremendous calls of God upon their lives were being attacked and seduced. The enemy had convinced them that it was just "too hard" to remain in the race, so they got out. I knew that this vision was not just for our own church but for the Church at large.

The vision further revealed a clear strategy of Satan. If he could seduce the supporters of ministry, then we would have no one to hold up our arms as Aaron and Hur did for Moses during the battle with the Amalekites (see Exodus 17:12–13). As a result, we as senior pastors would become weary and unable to go forth. The plans of our enemy became obvious: The thief would steal our leaders and servants, thus stealing our strength and support. With very few around to support us, we could not continue to be effective in ministry. Since we all are called to be leaders and servants in the Kingdom, this vision affects the entire Body of Christ.

The Devil's J-O-B

Did you ever wonder what the devil's real job is? I mean like his j-o-b—you know, the job where you punch a time clock and get paid to work? Yes, the 9-to-5 routine. Except the devil is at work 24/7!

In times past, when I would pray to strategize and develop counter-attacks, I thought he just showed up periodically with his "hit" list and then retreated for a while until it was time to smack me again. Similar to the Mafia, I believed Satan would have his network of crime lords, and when the evil godfather released his periodic hit lists all hell would break loose.

We observe in Scripture that his day *and* night job is to wear us out:

> And he shall speak great words against the most High, and shall *wear out* the saints of the most High, and think to change times and laws: and they shall be given into his hand until a time and times and the dividing of time.
>
> Daniel 7:25 (emphasis mine)

What does this actually indicate? It means our enemy will attempt whatever it takes to obtain such a hold on us that we will quit running the race and abort the fulfillment of destiny. He is compulsively focused and determined to exhaust us with long, weary battles, extensive spiritual warfare and seducing lies that threaten our relationship with God. All this is done to weaken our spiritual and physical strength and faith. He is diligent with his work schedule—it being both day and night—and he is completely dedicated to his cause. He even works during his lunch break, falsely accusing the saints before God. Friends, this guy never takes a vacation; he is dedicated to wearing us out. This is why it is extremely important that we understand his determination and rise up in spiritual warfare against him.

Know this one thing before we go further: We have already won the battle! The blood of Jesus has cleansed us and strengthened us to go forth into great victory. But in order to win, we must understand his tactics and the strategies of the head destiny thief. Every good soldier studies the maneuvers of his enemy in order to cut him off at the pass.

Jezebel and the Accuser Steal Destiny!

The accuser of the brethren is continually working with demonic governmental structures of evil authority to discredit the saints and undermine spiritual authority. The demonic assignments attempt to falsely accuse leaders and servants while at the same time stripping away their confidence. The members of the Body of Christ become convinced that they are ineffective and that God is unable to vindicate them from the vicious lies and rumors.

Once the sheep are wounded and inactive, an even greater bomb explodes: Jezebel hits her target! A Jezebel stronghold moves into the congregation to control the atmosphere through worship and intercession and prophetic ministry. Her main target is now the leaders as she attempts every known strategy to discredit them with false accusations and to undermine their authority. Preying upon the sheep, she seeks out the weak first, spreading lies and division. As most pastors can testify, this spirit attempts to stir up a congregation with strife, competition, false accusations and false prophecy. Only a short time passes before the church is split, or the leadership is torn apart, intercession is halted, and worship is stifled—all because a demon is simply doing his JOB.

The book of Revelation reveals that the accuser testifies falsely against the saints of God (see Revelation 12:10). The accuser's strategy is to promote disunity, which steals the life of any ministry. Since unity releases life, disunity releases death. Psalm 133 states that unity flows from the head down and that there is a release of greater anointing when the congregation is in unity. Since the anointing breaks off yokes of oppression, it is clear why the enemy plots to destroy the anointing. If there is no unity, then there is no anointing flowing to the Body of Christ.

> And it shall come to pass in that day, that his burden shall be taken away from off thy shoulder, and his yoke from off thy neck, and the yoke shall be destroyed because of the anointing.
>
> Isaiah 10:27

The only way to overcome this spirit of Jezebel is by proclaiming the blood of Jesus and the victory of the blood using our testimony against it. We also must love not our own lives unto death.

> And I heard a loud voice saying in heaven, Now is come salvation, and strength, and the kingdom of our God, and the power of his Christ: for the *accuser of our brethren* is cast down, which *accused them* before our God day and night. *And they overcame him by the blood of the Lamb, and by the word of their testimony; and they loved not their lives unto the death.*
>
> Revelation 12:10–11 (emphasis mine)

Victory in Blood

Each time we battle the accuser of the brethren, we lay down our lives once more and commit to the "higher calling" with a more determined effort. Since the devil desires to steal our destiny, the accuser hits hard and strategically targets every ministry dedicated to training the saints. Ministries with the mandate to fulfill Ephesians 4:11—those dedicated to training and equipping the saints—face an evil assignment of destruction.

We also must spiritually draw a "blood line" and declare that the enemy cannot step through the boundary of the blood of Jesus. We constantly have to declare the power of the blood of Jesus and remind the devil that we have the victory because of the blood. Many times I visit the sick in hospitals and take red ribbon with me. I deliberately cut the ribbon and tie it to their hospital beds as a sign of the bloodline being drawn in the spirit realm. We join together in prayer, plead the blood of Jesus Christ, draw the bloodline and command Satan and the spirits of death to leave the premises. As a result, God's power and anointing come and stay the hand of premature death. This is an example of a prophetic act that demonstrates a spiritual principle to the devil.

Victory in Testimony

Another area of victory is through our testimonies. We must continually remind the devil of what the Lord has done for us and testify of His goodness and His promises. In the middle of battle it is often difficult to focus on God's goodness, but when we press through to proclaim God's power and His Word, it breaks the assignment against us. We must understand that when the accuser comes, he wants to cause our minds to be confused and affect us to the degree that we feel we cannot testify about God's love and faithfulness. If we succumb to his pressure and believe his lies, then we cannot battle the accuser at all. At that very moment of crisis is when we need to be more determined to give our testimony. We must rise up and begin to declare the works of the Lord. Our testimony of His goodness will ensure the defeat of the accuser!

The Many Faces of Seduction

During the vision of the destiny thief and its planned seduction, I pressed in even further for more revelation. The Lord spoke very clearly that He was taking me on a journey to understand how the seducing spirit works through the accuser of the brethren, the Amalekite stronghold, the spirits of Jezebel and Belial and the unclean and religious spirits (all spirits are discussed later). He promised to release keys of understanding that would open up doors of victory, if only I would remain obedient to my own destiny to serve Him. This journey to understand the strategies of the enemy has taken several years, and revelation continues to unfold. One sure thing I have realized is that we must continually be determined for destiny and maintain the spirit of Caleb, or the seducing spirits will ensnare us at every turn. I have desired to quit the ministry more times than I care to mention. God has been faithful, however, to bring breakthrough after breakthrough, and I have remained determined to fulfill my destiny and take my mountain.

As I have pressed in for further revelation, I have become more and more encouraged. I have a renewed faith in His divine ability to deliver me from *all* oppression of my enemy. There is nothing too difficult for God (see Jeremiah 32:17). He and I make a majority, and as long as

I am obedient, all areas work together for my good (see Romans 8:28).

Our church survived another crisis, and we grew to new levels of faith and revelation. And oh, yes, we gained understanding of the destiny thieves, which is the reason for this book. Read on!

Two

Overcoming the "Perilous Times"

This know also, that in the last days perilous times shall come.

2 Timothy 3:1

Quick! Turn on the television in the bedroom! An airplane has crashed into the World Trade Center!"

My husband, Mickey, jolted from the bed. "What?" Half asleep, he grabbed his slippers and housecoat and made his way to the television.

The devastation of September 11, 2001, was televised on every possible channel and aired worldwide. Hearts across the nation sank with the newly discovered threats of terrorism.

For days the media committed to round-the-clock testimonies while the world anxiously waited for updated reports. Millions camped in front of televisions, totally fear-stricken, as terrorist assignments were unmasked. Many people even feared it to be "the end of the world." The tragedy stole the lives of loved ones, and millions of people grieved along with the families of the deceased.

The 9/11 tragedy was not limited to America; it was a calamity that affected the entire world. In fact, it literally "turned our world upside down." Fear wreaked havoc as millions of people panicked. It seemed as if the world actually stood still when airline travel and other methods of transportation were cut to minimums. Economic systems began to suffer and became even more crippled as the stock market took a downward spiral.

Terrorist threats manifested in new methods. Now we were aware of chemical warfare in a different dimension. Anthrax became a new word in our vocabulary. Suddenly our total environment—indeed, everything necessary to sustain life—was threatened. Our lakes and rivers, fields of grain, orchards, farmlands and even livestock all became possible targets for terrorists seeking to destroy us.

Troubled Times

We live in very perilous times, and the enemy thrives in fearful situations. In fact, he even devises plans against us to create fear.

The word *perilous* is a Greek word meaning "troubled." The *Enhanced Strong's Lexicon* goes further to translate the word as "dangerous to the point of being fierce and savage." It also states that the word relates to becoming slackened and relaxed and going from a higher place to a lower place.[1]

When we carefully examine 2 Timothy 3:1, we begin to gain revelation concerning the end times. Through word studies, it is clear that in the end times the enemy and his cohorts will release a savage onslaught that will be extremely fierce. I am sure you will agree that 9/11 was a fierce attack. But I believe it was much more than a terrorist assignment—it was also a demonic strategy of destruction. Seducing spirits are extremely active in our world today. Their plan is to strip us of all faith in God's ability to provide for us and cause us to focus on fear and tragedy.

Much of the enemy's fierce attack is targeted against the saints of the Most High. The assignment has been planned to be so very fierce that it persuades some to leave the faith or become lukewarm in their love for God. The enemy also seeks to seduce God's children into compromise, resulting in moving from higher places of authority to lower positions.

Is it any wonder that believers are consistently under attack? The devil wants to steal your destiny and authority! How many times have you known you have had a destiny of authority in God's Kingdom only to find yourself desiring to quit the race and run in the opposite direction?

Fulfilling the High Calling

Many of God's children are quitting the race! During these fierce and troubled times, pastors and other ministers are leaving their positions. Saints are compromising morality and integrity for fame and fortune. Some are settling for a lower call, a lower position and choosing a different route than what God has destined for each of them, which is the "high calling" of Christ. Philippians 3:14 states that we are to "press toward the mark for the prize of the high calling," and yet the enemy has pressured multitudes into settling for lower positions and defeated destiny.

To make this even clearer, allow me to show you step by step what happens during the seasons of "perilous times" as the enemy attempts to attack us:

1. It is a dangerous time.
2. It is so dangerous that the attacks from the enemy are fierce and even savage.
3. Seducing spirits are extremely active.
4. The enemy strategizes to seduce us into becoming slack and relaxed in our commitments to God.
5. If we do slack off or get relaxed, then we are removed from a higher to a lower place (in authority).

But we can take steps to overcome the perilous times (and attacks):

1. Pray!
2. Put on the full armor of God and take a firm combat position in spiritual warfare.
3. Activate your gift of spiritual discernment.
4. Use the keys of the Kingdom, binding all power of the enemy and loosing the perfect will of God.
5. Be on guard and spiritually alert at all times.
6. Become more committed to serve God.
7. Remain accountable to authority.
8. Do not compromise!

Satan, the False Prophet

During perilous times, a spirit of false prophecy will arise. This spirit often comes in a way you might not expect.

What do you think of when you imagine a false prophet? Do you envision a wild man who speaks as a loose cannon spouting weird words and prophecies that make no sense at all? Do you believe a false prophet is limited to someone who "misses it" while delivering a prophetic word? Well, dear ones, God wants to reveal to you that Satan himself falsely prophesies, especially during perilous and troubled seasons of your life. He speaks to your mind and seduces you to believe a lie and make unwise choices. He leads you in wrong directions and then persuades you to go his way rather than God's way. The enemy's voice may even seem like God's voice.

"What?!" I can almost hear some of you questioning that statement. You are most likely wondering how God and the devil could possibly sound alike. Well, actually they do not. The problem is that too many of us do not talk and listen to God enough to discern the correct voice.

Do Not Be Deceived!

Satan's voice is very seductive, and many times his voice is more familiar because we spend too much time listening to him. The Scripture states that Satan is transformed as an angel of light (see 2 Corinthians 11:14). Light is scripturally symbolic of truth. Therefore, according to God's Word, Satan's words sometimes sound like truth. If we are not properly trained to hear and discern the Father's voice, we can be deceived. Each of us must become committed to spiritual training so that we quickly recognize His voice. Through proper use of discernment we will not easily be seduced by the enemy to believe lies.[2] Spending more intimate time with the Father guarantees levels of accuracy in discerning the true light.

Many of God's children do not believe they can be deceived. I have been amazed at the number of Christians who fall prey to an angel of light. Even mature believers are vulnerable to this seducing spirit. We must all remain on guard, for Matthew states that false prophets will come to deceive the very elect.

> For there shall arise false Christs, and false prophets, and shall shew great signs and wonders; insomuch that, if it were possible, they shall *deceive the very elect.*
>
> Matthew 24:24 (emphasis mine)

There are many avenues of Satan's deception. Do not look for him to come as he did in the past, because he often chooses different doors. The devil lies in wait for the right time to attack us. He will seek any available entrance to abort destiny. Our job is to be on the alert: "Watch and pray, that ye enter not into temptation: the spirit indeed is willing, but the flesh is weak" (Matthew 26:41).

Church Prayer and Intercession

Perilous times provoke us to prayer. In fact, we will not survive the seduction of Satan if we are not watchful and in prayer. Be aware, however, that the devil hates prayer, and because it is so powerful he will strategize to dismantle prayer and intercession. Prayer reinforces spiritual intimacy and relationship with God, and the enemy hates that.

In the natural world, the result of intimacy between a husband and wife is pregnancy, when a seed is conceived. In the Spirit, when godly seeds are planted, there is a planned spiritual birthing. God desires to impregnate us with destiny and then empower us to fulfill our purpose. The enemy knows that during intimate seasons of prayer many seeds of destiny are planted within our spiritual wombs, and this is the very reason he sets his sight to dismantle prayer. The enemy's goal is to abort the destiny of Christ's Bride.

Our spirit is truly willing, but our flesh can be extremely weak under pressure. The enemy knows that if he can abort prayer, then he can weaken us. Prayer causes the spirit to become strong, just as the lack of prayer strengthens the fleshly nature. We must continually watch over our spirits, feeding our spirits with the Word of God and continuing to watch and pray so that the wicked one does not ensnare us.

And take heed to yourselves, lest at any time your hearts be overcharged with surfeiting, and drunkenness, and cares of this life, and so that day come upon you unawares. For as a snare shall it come on all them that dwell on the face of the whole earth. *Watch ye therefore, and pray always*, that ye may be accounted worthy to escape all these things that shall come to pass, and to stand before the Son of man.

Luke 21:34–36 (emphasis mine)

Using Spiritual Discernment

Matthew 12:29 reveals a spiritual principle given to all believers: "Or else how can one enter into a strong man's house, and spoil his goods, except he first *bind the strong man*? and then he will spoil his house" (Matthew 12:29, emphasis mine). The first important principle of spiritual discernment, then, is to bind the strong man.

The word *bind* in this passage is a Greek word meaning "to tie or fasten with chains."[3] In order to take spiritual authority over the strong man in operation, our first step is to tie him up with chains. These chains are words of prayer concerning our situations. We bind the enemy with revelation we receive from the Lord, and as we pray over circumstances we fasten chains around every demon that comes against us. The enemy therefore becomes imprisoned and unable to move in any intended direction. His planned strategies are suddenly negated, and we have the victory!

Just imagine: Every time you pray, another link is added to the chain that will bind the strong man. I pray that the chains you are using are l-o-o-o-ng chains. If your chain is not long enough, start praying now!

A second principle of spiritual discernment that is important for us to learn is to use the keys to the Kingdom given to us by Jesus Himself. He has not left us defenseless against the enemy. He gave us His name to use against Satan, and then He gave us the keys to the Kingdom.

> And I will give unto thee the keys of the kingdom of heaven:
> and whatsoever thou shalt *bind* on earth shall be bound in
> heaven: and whatsoever thou shalt loose on earth shall be
> loosed in heaven.
>
> Matthew 16:19 (emphasis mine)

These keys are instruments to unlock the gates of heaven
so that God's perfect will can be established on earth. Keys
of divine revelation are meant to become the keys that unlock heaven's gates for breakthrough.

We are commissioned to go up spiritually into the "high
places" of the Spirit with these keys of revelation and unlock doors that release spiritual breakthroughs. Every key
is simply a representation of divine revelation given to
us from God's own wisdom and knowledge. With divine
revelation, new levels of authority manifest. When we have
received fresh revelation we are empowered to use that
revelation as a key for breakthrough. Until we use our keys
of revelation with authority, we remain captives of Satan's
strategies.

Unless we continually bind the strongman, we are an
easy prey. It is always important, therefore, to discern the
spirit in operation during every attack of the enemy. Every
new assignment requires fresh discernment. By using our
keys, we open doors to victory.

Satan's Seat

I have realized that in specific seasons Satan gains a
"seat" of authority. Yes, Satan can gain a seat in our lives—a
foothold of power over any area we allow him to rule. This
foothold then becomes a throne.

Satan acquires a throne of authority wherever we allow
sin, doubt or unbelief. Obviously, where Satan gains a
seated position, he has a stronghold. The Scriptures speak

of Satan having a seat over the entire city of Pergamum. In Revelation 2 God addressed the church where "Satan's seat" (or throne) was established (see verse 13). Pergamum was under siege by this demonic assignment, yet the church there had not denied its faith.

God, however, had concerns against it. It upheld false doctrine, created stumbling blocks, ate foods sacrificed to idols and committed fornication (see verse 14). The church at Pergamum was rebuked for its idolatry and sin, and the Lord condemned it unless it chose to repent.

Satan had a throne in this first-century city, and he still has thrones today over individuals, businesses, churches, cities, countries, nations and governments. The same condemnation can occur in our own lives if we allow Satan to remain in his seated positions. Though we may confess Christ as our Savior and not deny our faith, very often we uphold false doctrines and belief systems, and we become stumbling blocks because of our sinful natures. Then Satan gains a stronghold.

In his seat of authority Satan plans to seduce the saints into areas of sin and apostasy in order to abort God's destiny for their lives. In the local churches, Satan continually attempts to enthrone himself through strife, division, gossip, murmuring and complaining. He seeks to do the same to entire nations. Unless repentance takes place, we easily become deceived, thus aborting our destinies.

Although Satan himself cannot be in more than one place at a time, he often releases authority to other principalities and rulers to do the work. Satan's seat of authority is often released through "territorial assignments."

Territorial Assignments

God gave me an enlightening pictorial analogy of Satan and his principalities executing a strategy over a territory.

One summer I visited my parents, who lived in the country on more than forty acres. In addition to their lovely personal home, the estate also had a very nice "getaway cottage" for my needed escape times. One summer evening while we rocked back and forth in the rocking chairs on the back porch of the little cottage and reminisced, a huge spider darted across the porch. This sudden attempt to cross to the other side of the porch caught my eye. My eyes focused on this hairy, unsightly thing—which appeared to be a tarantula. It was huge! And hairy! My brother-in-law grabbed the nearest broom, and with one swat the spider came to a sudden halt. Relieved, I took a deep breath, believing that to be the end of this life-threatening creature. Suddenly, hundreds of baby spiders fled for their lives, escaping in every direction. I could not believe my eyes. These baby spiders had been on their mother's back before her demise. Evidently she was transporting all her babies, and her back was the method of their transport. The spiders had piled up at least four spiders high, totally covering their mother's back, and she subsequently appeared to be ten times her normal size!

As I watched the tiny spiders flee in different directions, the Lord spoke to me concerning territorial spirits—those spirits assigned by Satan over large territories, such as cities, states or regions. They are strategic in their attempts to influence and seduce large amounts of people. These territorial spirits attempt to establish illegitimate satanic authority, or strongholds, over large areas. An example of a territorial stronghold is the principality to which Gabriel referred when he told Daniel he had encountered the prince of Persia (see Daniel 10:20).

The Lord revealed that the spider on my porch moved very similarly to a territorial demon. The larger, more powerful demons move into an area and "cover" that area with a stronghold. This dark, demonic, many-legged structure hovers over its assigned area with a strategic plan to steal the life from its victims. It carries with it hundreds of smaller demons.

Once this demonic army moves into its assigned territory, the strongman releases all the smaller demons to do their "work" upon the area. These may be spirits such as lying, perversion, legalism, pornography or even abortion—each with its own specific job to do. This is one way Satan gains seats in our communities, families, governments, etc.

This analogy of how Satan plans territorial assignments enlightened me for future spiritual warfare. I now realize that when I take authority over territorial spirits, I must discern which other demons have traveled with the main strongman. Then I go into prayer with more revelation and increased authority. Using the keys of the Kingdom and divine empowerment, I begin to bind the strongman who has a temporary stronghold.

Demonic Seated Positions Become Strongholds

Strongholds, put most simply, are well-fortified places in our minds that Satan has influenced. If Satan can defile our minds, then he can influence our belief systems, which in turn influence our actions. Doubt and unbelief begin to infiltrate our faith, and the results are bondage, spiritual imprisonment and an extreme lack of victory.

I firmly believe that in most situations the battle is in the mind. This is why we are encouraged to renew our minds and cast down every imagination (from the enemy) that exalts itself against the knowledge of God. Too often, in our minds, Satan has exalted his lies above God's plans and God's wisdom. By allowing an ungodly entrance into our minds, we choose to believe lies spoken from the enemy. We quickly receive unchallenged words of death, lies and deceit that Satan whispers into our ears. Unless we

49

challenge the negativity, these areas become well-fortified places—strongholds of Satan.

> Casting down imaginations, and every high thing that exalteth itself against the knowledge of God, and bringing into captivity every thought to the obedience of Christ; and having in a readiness to revenge all disobedience, when your obedience is fulfilled.
>
> 2 Corinthians 10:5–6

When Satan is able to plant his thoughts into our minds, then he has gained a seated position in our lives. In situations of bitterness and unforgiveness, for example, Satan gains a seated position. Other areas are desire for position and power, physical lusts and perversion that we never speak of but often think about. With the evil influences of sexual immorality promoted by Hollywood, Satan has gained a stronghold, a seated position that constantly defiles our minds and thought patterns. Seated positions in *any* area of our hearts become places for Satan to rule and reign over our lives.

Strongholds of Idolatry

 Every entrance allowed to Satan can easily become a seated position and a stronghold. Seated places become his place to abide, thus allowing him to rule and reign over people. One big entrance that allows Satan a stronghold is idol worship.

The inhabitants of Pergamum became influenced by the idols they worshiped. First Corinthians 10:20 exposes idol worship as devil worship. The idols are nothing, but the demons behind the idols are very real. When we worship idols, God's Word states that we worship devils. In other words, wherever there is idolatry there is a release of demonic activity. And whatever we worship, whatever we allow to become exalted over the exaltation of God, opens the door for the enemy to seat himself in that area and become empowered. If we choose to become disobedient and sinful, we open doors of demonic oppression and activity against us.

Many Christians do not realize they are opening doors to idolatry. Idolatry is not simply bowing down to a graven image. Idolatry is choosing to believe Satan's lies over God's Word. Remember, saints: <u>God and His Word are one.</u> They cannot be separated. <u>Believing the opposite of His Word is a form of idolatry.</u>

My 78-Pound Idol of Self

In my early twenties I suffered from <u>anorexia nervosa and bulimia.</u> I battled for seven years against the lying spirit that ruled and overpowered my will to live. Satan and his cohorts had seated positions in my life. Many days I felt as if I were driven by demons to exhibit extreme, bizarre behavior.

At 78 pounds, near death, the Lord began to set me free from demonic oppression. I later realized that I had been suffering the consequences of sin and idolatry. I did not actually bow down to an idol. I did not worship a Buddha or any graven image. I worshiped my body. My body image became more important than pleasing God, thus resulting in idolatry.

<u>Eating disorders are often rooted in control issues.</u> Like most anorexics, I wanted complete control of my life. I desperately needed to control my environment, my weight and every situation I might encounter. To prevent any perceived rejection, I remained in control through isolation. I would not leave my house for weeks except out of absolute necessity. I manipulated and maintained complete

control of *everything*. The eating disorder, however, began to control me.

The Lord revealed to me that the anorexic thought patterns and behavior were idolatry. At first I was shocked to realize that I was an idolater. Like many, I had the mind-set that idolatry involved graven images and bowing to them. But in reality, I was bowing down—I bowed low to the words of Satan concerning my life.

The devil deceived me, and I embraced false beliefs that God did not love me and that I was a mistake. I did not trust God, and that is the reason I decided to rule my own life. I chose to look to the world for acceptance and love. I felt that if I looked thin enough, I was in control. Satan uses that lie to destroy many of God's anointed. The lies attached to anorexia nervosa and bulimia are lies that steal our destiny.

Today I have the full realization that the Lord desires to be my complete source. I am to depend on Him for my identity and acceptance.

"Oh, I'm not an idolater!" you might also say. "I don't bow down to any graven image, and I am not a control freak."

I would encourage you to examine your heart. Are you obedient to follow the Lord totally? Do you put God first in your life? Do you spend time—quality time—with Him? If other "things" or "activities" take first place, then Satan may have a seated position in your life, just as he had in mine.

Dethroning Your Enemy through Dreams

In my recent book, *Dream On,*[4] I shared my testimony of how I was equipped through dreams and visions from God to overcome death and eating disorders. The Lord commissioned me to author *Dream On* for a twofold purpose. First, He wanted to emphasize the importance of dreams and visions and activate others in dream interpretation. Secondly, He wanted to help others realize that God desires to deliver them from strongholds through the revelations in their dreams. This is one very important way to dethrone the enemy.

Most everyone dreams, and most likely God is speaking to each of us through dreams and visions—yet we do not recognize His voice. One of the reasons for dreams and visions is to reveal hidden patterns of behavior and generational strongholds so we can experience freedom and deliverance. As we receive levels of revelation and deliverance, Satan also is dethroned from his seated positions in our lives!

If you are a dreamer, let me encourage you to seek information concerning God's voice. It is quite possible that even your destiny is being revealed by God speaking prophetically through your dreams.

The Church is in such transition that if we are not careful we will limit God's new thing. Most of us are crying out for the new wine. Though we do not wish to limit God, we still find ourselves wanting to control His Spirit. This is due to the fact that we really dislike change. We verbalize our desires for change, but we dislike the changes that take place! And because we are uncomfortable with the new, we often retreat to the old.

We must expect God to "break in on us" with dreams. Through godly dreams He can bypass the conscious mind and insert a dream, like adding a new computer chip, and speak truth to us. When we dream, we have absolutely no control, so God can speak and we cannot argue back! He will visit us in the night season and speak to us in our dreams to bypass religious mind-sets.

Start paying attention to your dreams. God is speaking!

A Final Way to Defeat the Thief

Another way to overcome a "destiny thief" is to proclaim the blood of Jesus over all sin and iniquity. Renounce the sin, rededicate your life to Jesus and repent for areas of defilement and uncleanness. Get back in the race and finish your course, and you will develop a powerful testimony that will destroy the enemy's foothold in your life. Ask God to reveal any religious mind-sets that block your ability to move forward with Him into your destiny and breakthrough.

Prayer

Father God, I repent for all areas of idolatry in my life. I ask that You forgive me for being a lover of self—selfish and self-centered. I have chosen my own way. I have chosen to follow the love of this life and the pleasures of this world over the love of Christ and His ways. I choose life this day. I choose to be an obedient vessel. Thank You for the blood of Jesus that cleanses me from all unrighteousness. Thank You for renewing my mind today. As I have repented, it removed the enemy from any seated place in my heart and life. I will continue to follow You and obey You in all my ways. I lay down my life for the sake of the Gospel. I will not compromise my stand for righteousness, and I will follow You all the days of my life. Empower me to remain a witness for Christ while on this earth. I use the keys of the Kingdom and bind the devil and all his plans against me in the mighty name of Jesus Christ. I choose to run my race and to finish the course You have given me. I thank You in advance for my deliverance from all oppression and evil plots against my destiny. In Jesus' name, Amen.

Three

Belial

And her adversary also provoked her sore, for to make her fret, because the LORD had shut up her womb.

1 Samuel 1:6

She made her way to the top of the Temple steps once again. Every step was an effort that day. She had not eaten for days; her sorrow and grief overrode her bodily hunger.

Just once more, Hannah told herself. *One more prayer to the Lord. Surely Jehovah will hear me this time.*

Her faith remained stable, even though she still had not experienced the fruits of her hopes for a child. Year after year she would pray in the Temple for a son, only to return home to disappointment.

Your consistent praying is a waste of time! Why do you weary yourself year after year begging your God for offspring? God will not answer you. Haven't you realized by now that your God has shut your womb? He has turned His back on you. You will never be worthy enough to be blessed! You may as well give up this hopeless cause. This was the voice of the beguiler. It was the same voice that seduced Eve hundreds of years earlier in the garden. The lying voice became more and more familiar as she remained in her weakened, emotional condition. At times it was difficult to discern if it was the beguiler or God speaking. Hannah was worn down with grief, which made it easy for deception to become a fortress of doubt and unbelief. Her exhaustion gave way for the accuser of the brethren to overpower her mind. There was a definite new sound in his voice; a sudden strength of persuasion that she could not deny—because now Belial was involved in the seduction. Belial had joined the teamed efforts for the total seduction of her mind, will and emotions.

Maybe God wants me to stop believing for a child. After all, I am one of those who appears never to get her breakthrough. I am cursed, and there is no amount of prayer that will change that. Hannah's thoughts had begun to align with the enemy's overpowering voice.

Hannah, you will never *have a child!* The seducing voices of Belial and the accuser grew louder as she pressed into the Temple.

With every step she would hear a third voice—that of Peninnah, her husband's second wife. Peninnah was blessed with children; Hannah was not. Though their husband, Elkanah, continued to give Hannah double portions and appeared to love her greatly, it was still not enough. External attention and blessings would never satisfy the barrenness she experienced. Only the blessing of conception would bring complete fulfillment.

"I have a heritage, and you don't." Peninnah's words were embedded in Hannah's mind. "You may receive more attention from our husband, but you will never be a mother. You will never experience the attention I receive, because I have given him many children."

Each recalled word from her adversary caused her more grief, but with every ounce of faith she continued to pray for her miracle.

"This time will be different." She fought for words of faith for a positive confession. "I will choose to believe that God will bless me. He will not leave me barren."

Uncontrollably, Hannah began to cry out loud. Finally empowered to prevail over the voice of the seducing spirit, she wailed so loudly that the priest in the temple had begun to observe her peculiar actions.

"I don't care what people think about me!" She began confessing beneath her breath, "I am going to touch God today with my prayers!" (I can easily identify with Hannah and the battle for her mind!)

Don't get too loud now, the sly, seductive voices whispered. *People know you will never have a child. The priest knows you will never have a child. You are wasting your time. What makes you believe God would listen to you?*

O God! Hannah cried out within herself. Her silent prayers chose never to give any place to the seductive spirits.

If You will give me a son, I will dedicate him to You! No razor will touch his head, and I will give him to You all the days of his life. She continued to voice these vows in her heart, never uttering an audible word.

Hannah was determined that she would never surrender her faith and agree with the familiar voice that tempted her to doubt her prayers. Her sorrow and lack of fulfillment were taking a backseat to her renewed faith and vision. With only her lips moving, she got the priest's full attention.

"Woman, don't you know you are not to come to the Temple drunk? How long have you been praying under the influence of the wine?" Eli asked.

Now look what you have done! The voice of Satan grew louder. *Run away! Stop your senseless praying. Now even the priests are making fun of your efforts. How can you expect God to believe your prayers? You are a worthless, cursed old woman. Good for nothing, that's what you are.*

The destructive voice pounded against her mind. *You are insignificant, ruined and marked with barrenness. What makes you believe that today's prayers are any different from the rest of your senseless petitions?*

Hannah pressed through her fear of rejection. For years she had persevered beyond the cutting words of Peninnah. Living in the same household with her adversary was almost unbearable. Her frailness was the result of grief due to her barren situation, having been so distraught and vexed by her adversary she was unable to eat. The familiar voice was constantly invading her faith and falsely accusing her. Yet she was able to reserve a portion of hope through it all. By the grace of God, she continued to believe God for the blessing.

Will it be different this time? Can it be different this time? Will God hear me? Like a broken record these thoughts replayed through Hannah's mind while Eli continued to drill her with questions and accusations.

Hannah's spirit arose within her as she continued to battle the foreboding voice of Belial. It was a wicked spirit. Even its name represented wickedness, good for nothing and worthless. Belial was a demonic influence that forecast and accomplished ruin and destruction upon victims that surrendered to its lies. With tremendous determination, Hannah stood strong in her faith.

"I am not drunk, only sorrowful!" Hannah firmly vindicated her actions. "I am pouring out my desires to the Lord. I am not wicked, nor a daughter of Belial." Her fortress of faith commanded a victory. She was persevering while holding her ground, still believing God would hear her prayers.

Eli gazed upon her countenance. Knowing this woman was touching the very heart of the Father, he blessed her. "Go in peace," he said, "and the God of Israel grant thee thy petition that thou hast asked of him" (1 Samuel 1:17).

The results of Hannah's determination removed Belial from his seated position. The spirit surrendered its stronghold, and Hannah was freed from the accuser's stratagem.

And Hannah shifted into her destiny and fruitfulness.

Wherefore it came to pass, when the time was come about after Hannah had conceived, that she bare a son, and called his name Samuel, saying, Because I have asked him of the LORD.

1 Samuel 1:20

The Destiny Thief Belial

The biblical account of Hannah and her conflict with barrenness is documented in the first chapter of 1 Samuel. It is the story of a godly woman who chose to fight in faith rather than retreat and surrender to hopelessness. Her adversary continually troubled her and provoked her to sorrow (see verse 6). Many times she could have chosen not to return to the Temple and pray for a son, but she continued to believe God would answer her prayers.

Can you relate to Hannah? Many of us have been barren and unfulfilled. Multitudes of God's children have cried out to fulfill destiny, only to be continually seduced and provoked to embrace doubt and unbelief. Hannah had the tenacity to press forward and continue to believe God. Battling the strongholds of Belial, she remained strong while believing God for her breakthrough.

Hannah made the confession to Eli that she was not giving place to the spirit of Belial. Out of her own mouth she identified the evil spirit behind the seductive voice of beguilement: "Count not thine handmaid for a daughter of Belial: for out of the abundance of my complaint and grief have I spoken hitherto" (1 Samuel 1:16).

The voice of Belial in Hannah's era is the same voice involved in today's spiritual seduction. The name *Belial* is another name for Satan. It is translated as "wicked, ungodly, evil, worthless and good for nothing." The name also means "to ruin; destruction; having lack; to wear out."[1]

At one time or another most of us will face the same foe as Hannah. Have you been experiencing extreme weariness while endeavoring to believe God for fruitfulness? Has the enemy attempted to seduce your thought patterns as he tried with Hannah? Have you heard a beguiling voice whispering into your thoughts statements similar to these?

- You are worthless!
- You are evil and ruined!
- You are wicked and good for nothing!
- God will never answer your prayers!
- You should be ashamed of yourself!
- You would be better off dead!

If you have heard these words, then there is a seducing, beguiling Belial spirit that is attempting to wear you out and wear you down. It is the same spirit that competed for a seat of authority in Hannah's thought patterns. The spirit of Belial is a demonic stronghold that reinforces patterns of shame. The spirit attempts to convince us that we deserve evil and that we will never measure up to the expectations of others. It also leads us to believe that we are always to blame for perceived failures.

Can you imagine the pain Hannah experienced? First she struggled with the shame of unfruitfulness—her inability to give her husband a son. Second, the humiliation and guilt she experienced because her husband's other wife could give him children made her feel even more useless and inadequate. Third, something inside Hannah confirmed that it was her destiny to have a child, yet that promise was not being fulfilled.

Most likely we all identify in some way with Hannah, believing there is more to life than what we are experiencing. When a spirit of Belial is active, however, the shame is unbearable, and the seduction of Belial's lies overwhelms our faith. A constant bombardment from the evil one wears us down, and we submit to the false belief that we are worthless and our circumstances will never change.

Because Belial is so persuasive and seductive in its tactics, some may even commit suicide. The result of hopelessness has proven totally devastating, causing even God's children to choose death over life. Belial targets in particular our children, and suicide is at an all-time high among teenagers.

We must lock into life! We must choose life. We must learn how to defeat the spirit of Belial. There is so much to live for—especially fulfilling destiny!

Belial's Seductions

Belial is mentioned in several other passages in Scripture. Studying these passages gives more insight into the specific seductions of Belial. Understanding this spirit's strategies of seduction helps us know how to pray and to engage him effectively in spiritual battle.

1. Idolatry

The Lord and His Word are one (see John 1:1), meaning He cannot be separated from His Word. Any beliefs or practices contrary to His Word are idolatry! Belial is a spirit of seduction that ensnares us into spiritual idolatry and harlotry.

61

Deuteronomy 13:13 specifically mentions the children of Belial as those who are influenced by strongholds of idolatry:

> Certain men, the children of Belial, are gone out from among you, and have withdrawn the inhabitants of their city, saying, Let us go and serve other gods, which ye have not known.
>
> Deuteronomy 13:13

Not only are they themselves seduced by Belial, but also they seduce others to embrace lifestyles of wickedness and idolatry. They say, "Come with us! Go our way, and we will serve other desires." It is similar to Satan baiting a hook and tossing it in our direction, hoping we will swallow his bait. In other words, it is a form of spiritual seduction.

2. Illegitimate Authority

One way Belial uses idolatry and seduction in today's churches is through a person (or group of people) who attempts to gather others to himself/herself. This is a self-proclaimed leader who administrates power through illegitimate authority. Because of an offense or a lack of personal recognition, he seeks others to come to his "side." The strategy is to gain influence and power by falsely accusing spiritual authority and to control and manipulate by the twisting of words in an attempt to destroy unity.

Such self-proclaimed leaders guide others through doors of rebellion, serving the gods of their own fleshly desires of control and power. We may not understand these methods as "idolatry," but any religious system and structure that is above the principles and character of Christ is idolatry.

The Lord rebukes those who heed and give a seat of authority to the destructive spirit of Belial. God is most specific in commanding His children to utterly destroy all who are influenced by this stronghold. Let us study further Deuteronomy 13:

> If thou shalt hear say in one of thy cities, which the LORD thy God hath given thee to dwell there, saying, Certain men, the children of *Belial*, are gone out from among you, and have withdrawn the inhabitants of their city, saying, Let us go and serve other gods, which ye have not known; then shalt thou inquire, and make search, and ask diligently; and behold, if it be truth, and the thing certain, that such abomination is wrought among you; thou shalt surely smite the inhabitants of that city with the edge of the sword, *destroying it utterly*, and all that is therein, and the cattle thereof, with the edge of the sword.
>
> Deuteronomy 13:12–15 (emphasis mine)

The seductiveness of Belial was such a detriment to Israel that God gave specific instructions to destroy everyone who allowed Belial to remain in a seated position of authority—all the inhabitants of that entire city. The commandment of destruction even included destroying all the cattle! No evil influence of the Belial nature was to be left living. The Israelites were to take the idols and burn them with fire and destroy the city. It was forbidden for Israel to partake of the spoils. If they disobeyed and took the spoils, then they were convicted of taking "cursed" things (verse 17). Through this passage God is specifically instructing us not to give heed to Belial's voice or those in agreement with this spirit.

For us today, this requires the cleansing fire of the Holy Spirit to burn away the agreements made with this enemy. If we repent and turn from our wickedness, He will be faithful to cleanse and heal our land (see 2 Chronicles 7:14).

3. Homosexuality

In Judges 19:22 the sons of Belial demanded sexual relations with another man. The master of the house refused to allow his guest to be shamed in such a manner, so he offered his daughter to the evil men to abuse sexually:

> Now as they were making their hearts merry, behold, the men of the city, certain sons of Belial, beset the house round about, and beat at the door, and spake to the master of the house, the old man, saying, Bring forth the man that came into thine house, that we may know him. And the man, the master of the house, went out unto them, and said unto them, Nay, my brethren, nay, I pray you, do not so wickedly; seeing that this man is come into mine house. . . . Here is my daughter a maiden, and his concubine; them I will bring out now, and humble ye them, and do with them what seemeth good unto you: but unto this man do not so vile a thing.
>
> Judges 19:22–24

The stronghold of this evil spirit is so powerful that it can even persuade a father to offer his own daughter to be abused in such a vile way.

Remember that the name *Belial* means "wicked, ungodly, evil; to ruin; destruction."[2] Taking these definitions into consideration, it is obvious that it is the spirit of Belial that Paul mentions in 2 Timothy 3:1–3, and that this spirit will manifest as sexual perversion in the end times:

> This know also, that in the last days *perilous times* shall come. For men shall be lovers of their own selves, covetous, boasters, proud, blasphemers, disobedient to parents, unthankful, unholy, *without natural affection*, trucebreakers, false accusers, incontinent, fierce, despisers of those that are good.
>
> 2 Timothy 3:1–3 (emphasis mine)

4. Rebellion

Belial labors with, and may even foster, rebellion. In 2 Samuel 20 we read that the stronghold of Belial entered the heart of a man named Sheba. Sheba led a rebellion against

King David and had to be slain—utterly destroyed—to keep peace in David's army.

How many times have we witnessed the influence of Belial operating within the local church? The stronghold of rebellion is constantly manifesting in attacks against godly authority through slander, false accusations and rebellion. This spirit has to be addressed and prayed against. It must be ostracized and rendered helpless by giving it no place or authority within the church.

To preserve corporate unity in David's army, everyone in agreement with the spirit of Belial had to be destroyed. Think of this in terms of the corporate church. Discipline is necessary when there are attempts to disrupt unity, or the result is spiritual and corporate defilement.

5. Stealing Your Inheritance

In 1 Kings 21, Queen Jezebel's husband, Ahab, was king of Israel, and he strongly desired the vineyard of a man named Naboth. Naboth wanted to maintain ownership of the vineyard because it was his inheritance. One day Ahab pouted and cried to Jezebel about the vineyard. Jezebel manipulated circumstances to steal the vineyard from Naboth. She set two sons of Belial to falsely testify against Naboth. As a result Naboth was murdered, and Ahab illegally acquired the vineyard. In this passage we recognize Belial personified as Satan: the lying, seducing, beguiling, unclean, murdering stronghold.

Today we witness the same spirit falsely accusing others. The spirit manifests in the identical manner of the past, seducing believers into sins of the flesh, spiritual wickedness, doubt and unbelief, sexual perversion, lies and deceit, rebellion, slander, false accusations and even murder. Obviously Belial cohabitates with another destiny thief, the spirit of Jezebel, while attempting to steal all our inheritance—just as they did to Naboth.

Saints, if you are giving any place to Belial and/or Jezebel, then your entire future is threatened! Your intended destiny and inheritance is at risk if you allow Satan to occupy a seat in your life. You must take steps to utterly destroy all. In other words, stop now and ask God to open your heart to any needed correction. Utterly destroy anything God says displeases Him. (In the following chapters, we will discuss further the concept of utterly destroying all that is contrary to God's Word.)

Protect your inheritance!

6. Selfishness and Self-Centeredness

I have never understood fully why so many Christians remain self-centered. As believers, we should be more concerned for the welfare of others than for ourselves, but all too often godly people remain in patterns of self-centeredness and codependency. Because it is our destiny to win souls for Christ and to be concerned for the lost, it bothers me why many Christians remain stagnant in their concern for others. Choices are made to remain in areas of "woundedness" and "victimization," rather than reaching out and ministering to others in need. After searching the Scriptures, I realized that King David dealt with the same problems of self-centeredness—within his own army!

In 1 Samuel 30, King David had just achieved a tremendous victory. David had left the weak soldiers behind and did not force them into battle. This was a wise decision, for he would have forfeited their lives because of their weakened condition. In the battle against the wicked Amalekites, David and his army were empowered to overtake their enemy and recover all that had been stolen. Because David's heart was unified with his people, he desired to share the victory and the spoils with everyone, including the weak soldiers who had not fought in the battle. David displayed the heart of a true leader.

Belial, however, was at work among David's men after their great defeat of the Amalekites. Even after a great victory, the seduction of selfishness and self-centeredness, along with greed, manifested through the soldiers. They were referred to as the men of Belial, and they did not want to share the spoils of battle. (Here we identify two strongholds working together: the Amalekites and Belial.)

> And David came to the two hundred men, which were so faint that they could not follow David, whom they had made also to abide at the brook Besor: and they went forth to meet David, and to meet the people that were with him: and when David came near to the people, he saluted them. Then answered all the wicked men and *men of Belial*, of those that went with David, and said, Because they went not with us, we will not give them ought of the spoil that we have recovered, save to every man his wife and his children, that they may lead them away, and depart.
>
> 1 Samuel 30:21–22 (emphasis mine)

David realized that even though some of his men were left behind, they remained a valid part of the army. The men of Belial, on the other hand, were only concerned about themselves, their own sacrifices and their self-promotion. Belial attempts to influence others into believing that their success is due to personal charisma and their own gifting, with no thought of others who sacrificially gave in order for that leader to achieve success.

7. Spiritual Barrenness

We each have a predetermined destiny to birth something more than what we are presently experiencing. But the spirit of Belial wants to prevent that birth; it wants to keep us in spiritual barrenness. So the spirit of Belial not only lies to us, but also it seduces us to believe and agree with any lie that would cancel our destiny. Belial seeks a seated position in our lives through distortions of truth and false belief systems. Its aim is to seduce us into believing the very opposite of what God has said using counterfeit words that counteract His promises. This is spiritual barrenness.

The spirit of Belial applies extreme pressure to wear us out. Once exhausted and vulnerable, we are forced to give up any footing gained. As a result, the enemy moves in for the "kill." After all hope is destroyed and all joy has departed, the vulture, Satan, swoops down upon us to kill, steal and destroy.

The Word states that perilous times represent times of violence and fierceness. A vulture is fierce in its kill. It circles over and over, waiting for its prey to die, then swiftly swoops down upon its victim, sometimes before it is completely dead. A vulture picks its victim apart, piece by piece, until its appetite is satisfied.

When Belial fiercely attacks, we often feel dead and lifeless as our vision is blocked. If we quit running the race and give up in despair, the results are more barrenness and lack of fulfillment. When vision for destiny is lost or even postponed we not only lose hope, but also we can easily perish! Losing destiny vision and hope often ends in spiritual death.

In my husband's recent book, *Regaining Vision*,[3] he reveals that loss of vision is similar to a ship not having a rudder. The ship has no definite direction; it is simply tossed to and fro by adverse waves. When our destiny is robbed or stolen, we are easily tossed back and forth from one wind of adversity to another with no determination to achieve or to accomplish a goal.

If Hannah had lost her vision permanently, she also would have lost hope to press onward. But when the Word of the Lord finally came, she was empowered to hope once more, her vision was restored, she overcame spiritual barrenness, and Belial was defeated.

Strategies for Overcoming Belial

We can overcome the destructive spirit of Belial through the power of the Holy Spirit. With Christ's power working through us, we can be set free from Belial's evil power and press forward into new life in Christ, thus walking into our destinies. Let's consider several strategies to overcome Belial's influence in our lives.

1. Be Determined to Fight for Your Blessings

Hannah held fast to her faith in God. She had a destiny, and she was determined to receive her blessing. Though tempted to abandon her hopes for a male child, she continued to cry out to God for her blessing. We must be determined to do the same.

Hannah was much like Jacob, who struggled for the blessings of God. Jacob wrestled with the angel of God until he possessed his breakthrough. In fact, he wrestled all night and refused to let go of God until he received the blessing. Can you imagine this type of determination—wrestling with the angel of the Lord? What boldness! What determination! What faith!

Just picture Jacob, wallowing in dirt and weeds all night long. He was most likely weary from the night's adventure, yet he chose to hold on until he received his heart's desire. He sacrificed his sleep, his energy and comfort to get the victory. Jacob had made up his mind that it was time for a change. Up to this point, he had been a liar and deceiver. In fact, his name, *Jacob*, means "supplanter and schemer."[4] Now all alone with no one near to help him, he met God face-to-face. Jacob decided that the old had passed away and the time had arrived for his "new thing"! That new thing was a new name and the blessings of God spoken over his life. And his perseverance paid off because during that wrestling match, God changed his name from *Jacob*, "the supplanter," to *Israel*, "the prince of God." Wow! Talk about a shift!

Hannah's destiny was to birth a son, Samuel, who was to become a mighty prophet of God. Israel's destiny was to be the father of a nation consecrated unto God. It is important to recognize that the destinies of both of these mighty people of God were linked to the destinies of their children, their children's children, and so on. We are all connected in the Body of Christ. When one of us reaches our destiny, another will reach his. This is a good reason to pray for each other.

Yes, each of us has a destiny. We will have to fight for our breakthroughs and destiny just as Hannah and Jacob fought for their fulfillment.

2. Have Faith in the God of the Possible

As stated earlier, we each have a predetermined destiny to birth something more than what we are presently experiencing. In the natural it may seem impossible. But as children of God we must press into the supernatural realm of the possible. Our God is the God of the possible. All things are made possible through our Lord: "And Jesus looking upon them saith, With men it is impossible, but not with God: for with God all things are possible" (Mark 10:27). Though we may be barren, we must be determined to believe for the impossible to manifest as the possible.

Don't give up on God's promises! Never quit believing that God will bless you. Be like Hannah and Jacob and believe God to release you from your barren situations.

3. Realize That Your Strength Lies in Warfare

Your strength and your ability to defeat Belial lie in your determination to war over your inheritance. It is time for each of us to come out of the wilderness.

Song of Solomon 3:6 speaks of the bride coming out of the wilderness: "Who is this that cometh out of the wilderness like pillars of smoke, perfumed with myrrh and frankincense, with all powders of the merchant?" This is a passage describing the wedding procession, and the king is awaiting his bride. Symbolically, it represents Jesus awaiting His Bride, the Church. His Bride has been prepared. Though she has been in the wilderness—the season of her life that has cleansed and purified her in every way—she finally is coming out to meet her king.

The biblical account of Esther describes how she was mentored and "made ready" for twelve months to approach the king. For a solid year she was bathed in oils and perfumes. She was purified with myrrh for six months. During her time of preparation Esther did not enjoy lavish, "Calgon-take-me-away" soakings. She was not simply oiled down or sprayed with perfume like today. Rather, the myrrh was scrubbed into her skin to become a part of her—so that she herself became a sweet-smelling fragrance.

Isn't this similar to what God desires in each of us as His Bride? He wants us to be that pure fragrance—not just a sweet smell that dissipates in a few hours. He rubs us with His hand to purify and cleanse us in our preparation to meet the Bridegroom. (We will learn more about Esther and her significance in chapter 8.)

Defeating Belial requires coming out of the wilderness prepared, having fought for our inheritance and won. Like the bride of Solomon, like Esther, we must come through the wilderness anointed, cleansed and purified. We must emerge victorious from the spiritual wilderness ready to meet our King!

4. Be a Covenant Warrior

Behold his bed, which is Solomon's; threescore valiant men are about it, of the valiant of Israel. They all hold swords,

71

being expert in war: every man hath his sword upon his thigh because of fear in the night.

Song of Solomon 3:7–8 (emphasis mine)

This passage states that around Solomon's bed are armed men of war. Who would ever imagine that a king would desire armed soldiers surrounding his marriage bed? The bed represents covenant relationship, which implies receiving our inheritance based on the covenant promises from intimacy with Christ. The armed soldiers are symbolic of the spiritual warfare needed in this season.

The only way we will receive the covenant blessing is through warfare. Notice that the soldiers' swords are not drawn but are at their thighs. The thigh represents strength and reproduction. In other words, our strength to possess our promises and to be delivered from spiritual barrenness lies in our determination to war over our promised inheritance.

Most of us are weary of warfare, but we cannot quit fighting the enemy. Remember Caleb? He was eighty years old and still fighting! He endured the wilderness, that desert place where he was being prepared for his covenant promise, and then he came out with an increased determination to receive God's blessings and promises.

Saints, it is time for war. Don't back down! We are destined for fruitfulness. We must be like Caleb and declare, "Give me my mountain!"

Ways to Recognize Belial at Work

1. Physical attacks and weakness; being worn out
2. Generational spiritual wickedness
3. Overwhelming shame and hopelessness
4. Lies, uncontrollable thoughts of despair and failure
5. Thoughts of suicide and self-destruction

6. Recognizing a thief in your finances or losing your inheritance
7. False accusations
8. Selfishness, self-centeredness and greed
9. Lust, perversion, unclean thoughts and patterns of behavior
10. Idolatry in any form
11. Being lazy, lukewarm and compromising
12. Illegitimate authority; unable to submit to and trust authority
13. Natural or spiritual barrenness
14. Negativity

How to Pray a Prayer of Deliverance and Repentance

1. As you begin to pray, renounce any or all the ways you have agreed with Belial's lies.
2. Ask the Lord to forgive you for each of the areas of sin.
3. Be specific in renouncing each generational pattern.
4. Ask God to forgive your ancestors and yourself for allowing Belial to have a seat of authority.
5. Choose to forgive yourself and others for the sins and consequences of the sin.
6. Renounce any ungodly beliefs that you have concerning yourself and others.
7. Break covenant with the lies of Belial with which you may have agreed.
8. Agree with God's Word and what He declares over your life.
9. Thank the Lord for the blood of Jesus, which cleanses you and places you in right standing for your promised inheritance!

Four

Purge Out the Leaven!

Know ye not that a little leaven leaveneth the whole lump?

1 Corinthians 5:6

One cup of flour, one teaspoon of baking powder, one-half cup of shortening and one teaspoon of soda. Mix it all together in a bowl and what do you have? Absolutely nothing but some lifeless ingredients. If you are hoping for bread, you must add the yeast. Upon adding this magic ingredient, a multiplication process begins—you suddenly have an "alive" substance. Yeast is an ingredient that not only causes fermentation in wine but also is a source of reproduction. The yeast actually reproduces itself through agitation, meaning that the combination of yeast and other ingredients causes a reaction that releases the multiplication.

After a measure of time the combined substances become what is commonly referred to as a lump of dough. Now you can take the dough, knead it several times, form a loaf and place it into the oven. After the baking process you will have delicious bread.

By simply adding the one single ingredient of yeast, the mixture rises and forms the lump. Without it, there is no increase or expansion within the lump to make leavened bread.

Christ used the symbol of yeast to explain how just a little amount of sin can multiply into a whole "lump" of sin. The apostle Paul addressed the Corinthians concerning their sins and said that they needed to get rid of even the least amount of leaven so that the entire Church would not be seduced by the sin. Just a little leaven (yeast) multiplies quickly, and before you realize it the entire congregation is in sin. And the more agitation that occurs, the more leaven is created—and the more sin will abound.

The Scriptures contain several examples of what I call positive multiplication. God commanded us, for example, to be fruitful and multiply (see Genesis 1:22, 28). This is positive multiplication. Deuteronomy 32:30 states that when one prays it puts one thousand to flight, but when two pray it puts ten thousand to flight! Another example is giving. When we give offerings to God, the Word says they are multiplied back to us (see Luke 6:38). This is God's type of positive multiplication: an exponential increase.

Obviously, if you desire expansion like the rising necessary in making bread, this is a desired multiplication! But if it is the leaven, or the yeast, referred to in Scripture as sin, then it is an undesired multiplication.

The enemy is always quick to attempt a seduction. He causes agitation among the sheep and then sits back and observes the results of its multiplication. If he can manifest through a saint to spread gossip and slander, for example, then the multiplication process begins. Gossip will be on the "rise" as yeast to flour, and soon an entire lump of strife and division is formed within the Body of Christ.

The apostle Paul encouraged believers to purge out the old leaven so they might become a new lump and free of sin. By admonishing them to become unleavened, they would be free of defilement, malice and wickedness.

> Your glorying is not good. Know ye not that a little leaven leaveneth the whole lump? Purge out therefore the old leaven, that ye may be a new lump, as ye are unleavened. For even Christ our passover is sacrificed for us: therefore let us keep the feast, not with old leaven, neither with the leaven of malice and wickedness; but with the unleavened bread of sincerity and truth.
>
> 1 Corinthians 5:6–8

At the time Israel was released from Egypt, the Lord instructed them to eat only unleavened bread. During each future Passover celebration, Israel was to remember their exodus from Egypt by eating the unleavened bread. This was symbolic of Israel being separated from Egypt and removed from the bondage of sin. The Red Sea crossing was symbolic of death to the old man and being baptized through Christ into the new life. Due to the blood sacrifice of Christ Jesus, our sins are washed away and we become new creatures.

The Ways That Yeast Multiplies

God's Word instructs us to refrain from negative reports, association with idolaters and the filth of moral sin. If we do not, then we are allowing yeast to multiply in our lives. Let's take a look at the primary ways that yeast multiplies.

1. Negative Reports

As a former pastor and present leader, I do not believe God's children fully understand the effects of negativity and negative reports—especially how these affect a church congregation. If we fully perceived the damage negativity has upon our destinies, we would remain positive and watch every single word uttered from our mouths!

I have easily related to Moses, the Israelites' pastor in the wilderness, because he saw the immediate effects of a negative report from members of his congregation. Do you remember in Numbers 13 when Moses sent the twelve spies into Canaan? Moses gave instructions to spy out the land and to study the surroundings. The task Moses gave the twelve was to focus not on the strength of the giants, but to return with details of strategy to defeat the giants. Moses knew there would be warfare. His plan was not to determine if they would take the land, but to strategize how they would take it.

Let's study the strategy of Moses' commissioning. He was sending the twelve forth as a reconnaissance team—a group that moves into a territory, studies the natural surroundings and then sizes up the strengths of the enemy. Following those steps, a plan is then devised of how to overcome the strengths and make them weaknesses. There is never to be an option as to whether or not they are to take the territory.

Moses' instructions to the spies were to study the land and determine if it was good or bad, fat or lean, wooded or barren (see Numbers 13:20). More details were required of the spies, such as evaluating the people and how many occupied Canaan. They were to report on the cities—whether they were walled or open.

The twelve crossed quietly over the Jordan and sneaked into Canaan to spy out the territory. They returned after forty days. Does the number forty sound familiar? Many

Scriptures refer to the number forty. Moses was in the desert for forty years; Jesus was tested for forty days; and Noah endured the flood for forty days and nights. This particular number is symbolic of testing. Think about this: Israel had forty days to overcome negativity and return with a positive attitude.

Of all the items they could have carried back for the nation of Israel to see, they chose to bring grapes—big grapes! The cluster of grapes was so large that they had to carry the grapes on a staff to equalize the weight between two men. Wow! Can you imagine ordering a fruit plate for dinner that night? Just one grape would probably cover an entire plate!

Often I have wondered why they chose to bring back the fruits of the land and accompany the good of the land with a negative report. They could have returned with several stones from a well-fortified wall, a description of the gates of the cities, the armor of a soldier or a description of the hills, valleys and watering holes. Instead they brought back fruit. They used wisdom by focusing on the fruit and bringing it to show the people the fruits of the land—but they followed it with a negative report. It was like saying, "Look at this luscious fruit, look at the giant clusters, gaze upon the ripeness of this harvest. And there is more—so much more—waiting for us. But we cannot have any of it because giants occupy the land!"

Talk about a setup! It sounds just like the devil and how he lies to us today. We hear messages about breakthroughs, about how much God desires to increase our finances, heal us and bless us. We begin to visualize the breakthrough. We can taste the victory. Then the devil speaks into our ears and says, "But it is not for you! Don't you know that miracles died with the apostles? Don't you know you will never be blessed?" If we choose to listen to the negative report of the enemy, we will focus on the giants that block our breakthroughs. And we will never receive those breakthroughs.

By studying the twelve spies sent by Moses into Canaan, we gain understanding of how a negative report from only ten people can defile an entire nation. The negativity of the few became the "yeast" or "leaven" that affected all Israel.

Joshua and Caleb, however, returned to Moses with a positive report. These two brave spies stood before all Israel and proclaimed that they were well able to take the land. They encouraged Israel to focus on the fruit and to believe the Word of the Lord.

Choosing not to believe God has consequences. Because the rest of Israel chose not to believe the positive report of Joshua and Caleb, they died in the wilderness. An entirely new generation of believers was raised up to cross over the Jordan and possess their Promised Land. The ones who died would have received the blessing if only they had rid themselves of the leaven, had destroyed it and had chosen to listen to the report of the Lord.

If we choose not to rid ourselves of the leaven and utterly destroy all, then we will suffer the same results as Israel. In a church, negativity can split a congregation, discourage leaders, cause strife and division and steal vision. Negative words lead to gossip and slander. Murmuring and complaining run amuck and rob the faith of the people. Doubt and unbelief manifest within a negative environment. Pastors become so discouraged that they leave the ministry and must be replaced with a novice. How can someone with little experience fill the shoes of a seasoned, quality leader? The sheep begin to scatter because they lack trust, backsliding begins, and the Church remains in the wilderness.

So many times we are seduced into believing that our giants are too big. Saints, if God says to believe that we are able to overcome the giants that stand before us, we need to lock our faith into His promises. The Word of God gives specific instructions that we are to set our faces like flint toward destiny and to keep our eyes on the prize (the fruit!).

2. Idle Words (Shut Up and March!)

We must watch over our words. Scripture warns us that we will give an account for every idle word.

> A good man out of the good treasure of the heart bringeth forth good things: and an evil man out of the evil treasure bringeth forth evil things. But I say unto you, That every idle word that men shall speak, they shall give account thereof in the day of judgment.
>
> Matthew 12:35–36

 An *idle* word translates as "barren" and "lazy."[1] This means that idle words are a result of laziness in not watching over our words. It also means that those words are barren. When we speak forth lazy words, they are totally lifeless and unproductive. As a result, the enemy twists the words and multiplies them into negativity.

Remember when Joshua had to march around Jericho? The entire army could not talk until the final trip around the city. They had twelve silent trips around the city to rid themselves of negativity. On the thirteenth trip only a shout of victory could be released. Could it be possible that in order to quench any possible negativity we need to go into battle closemouthed? This may be a lesson for all of us if we want an assured victory.

3. Having a Better Idea than God's

God told King Saul to go into battle against the Amalekites and to destroy every living person—man, woman and child—and every living animal—even the sheep. God was very specific:

> Now go and smite Amalek, and *utterly destroy all* that they
> have, and spare them not; but slay both man and woman,
> infant and suckling, ox and sheep, camel and ass.
>
> 1 Samuel 15:3 (emphasis mine)

But Saul had a better idea. He spared Agag, the king of the Amalekites, along with a vast multitude of livestock. Saul did destroy what he considered vile and refuse. But what Saul considered good was not *utterly destroyed*, as God had commanded. Saul set himself in a position to determine what good and bad were, not heeding what God indicated was clean and unclean, good and bad.

The disobedience Saul displayed greatly grieved God to the point that God repented for allowing Saul to be king (see 1 Samuel 15:11). The prophet Samuel became so grieved over Saul's actions of disobedience that he cried to the Lord all night. Samuel arose the next morning knowing he had to speak prophetic words of rebuke and chastisement.

When Samuel confronted Saul, he realized the king's denial was his sin. King Saul proclaimed that he had performed the commandment of the Lord. Rather than dis-playing a repentant heart, Saul attempted to cover his sin and indicated that he had followed God's instructions. Samuel responded that he still heard the bleating of the sheep and the lowing of oxen, which proved that all had not been utterly destroyed. The prophet Samuel obviously was anointed to expose sin, and Saul was caught "red-handed" in his sin of disobedience. How could he vindicate himself? How could he retreat from this direct exposure?

Have you heard the expression "up the creek without a paddle"? I believe that is how Saul felt when the prophet of God directly addressed his sin. Samuel did not back down from his position as a prophet. He directly addressed Saul's disobedience, and Saul began to look for a paddle to go back downstream to a safer place!

Saul's "better idea" was nothing more than direct disobedience to God. And this disobedience later resulted in God's taking the kingdom away from him. So Saul ultimately forfeited his destiny.

4. Playing the Blame Game

Blaming others seemed like a good idea for vindication, so Saul told Samuel that "they" brought the animals from the Amalekites and "the people" spared the best of the sheep and oxen. After all, it was for the sacrifice to God. But the rest of the animals, Saul tried to convince Samuel, were "utterly destroyed" (1 Samuel 15:15).

I have heard many pastors minister on the subject of denial and have made jokes concerning the subject. One common one is "Denial is not a river in Egypt" (implying the Nile). But denial is a serious sin. *Denial* means "refusing to accept responsibility for a wrong action or refusing to believe what is true." You might recall someone in your life who denies he is wrong or refuses to recognize fault. How many times have we denied our sin or blamed others for our wrong decisions? Problems only multiply when we refuse to face reality or to accept responsibility for sin.

Saul denied his actions for not utterly destroying all. He denied his sin. Then he blamed others for going against God's plan and would not accept or admit his responsibility for the actions.

Samuel confronted Saul's disobedience a second and third time, but Saul insisted that he obeyed God's voice and answered again in the same way: "But the people took . . . the chief of the things . . . to sacrifice unto the LORD thy God" (verse 21). Saul's denial required strong chastisement; therefore, God removed him from his position as king.

83

Only then did Saul repent for his sin. Verse 24 says that Saul finally admitted that he "feared the people, and obeyed their voice." Saul begged God's forgiveness, but the repentance came too late, for God had already taken the kingdom from Saul and had given it to another person (see verse 28).

What Is Not Destroyed Rises Up to Destroy Us!

God instructed Saul to utterly destroy all for a specific purpose. God knew that if the Amalekites were not totally destroyed, they would rise up at a later date and destroy Israel.

Years after Saul's disobedience in not utterly destroying the Amalekites, it was an Amalekite who took Saul's crown. In Saul's final battle he fell upon his own sword, and an Amalekite witnessed his death and took Saul's valuables. Since the crown was most likely valuable and jeweled, it was probably taken as well. Later the Amalekite thief informed King David of the tragic death of Saul, thinking David would be pleased. But King David was very discerning and had the Amalekite destroyed (see 2 Samuel 1:1–16).

If leaven is not utterly destroyed, it rises up and makes a lump. If sin is not utterly destroyed, it rises up and makes an "unholy lump." This is why we must allow God to lay His axe to our unholy root systems. If we do not embrace the fire of His purity, our sin will rise up and destroy us, as it did to Saul. Disobedience in refusing to destroy all unclean areas of the flesh could culminate in our future destruction.

We must become as King David. We must be discerning and destroy every Amalekite spirit that stands in our way.

We Must Not Make an Unholy Alliance

Saul compromised and made an alliance with the king of the Amalekites, and his destiny was aborted. From the time of the compromise, barrenness was put in motion. The results of disobedience and rebellion are always barrenness.

Our adversary is a liar and the father of all lies. We must never make any alliance with the devil. We must be like David who was discerning at all times and destroyed the strongman in operation.

Choices Determine Destiny

Often I have wondered how Saul's history would have changed if only he had chosen obedience. How would the Bible read if he had chosen to utterly destroy all? How would the history of Israel have changed if the king had chosen obedience over sacrifice?

How would your history have changed if you had chosen obedience in past situations? Our future, just like Saul's, is determined by past obedience.

Destiny is the result of past choices. Many times we are not walking in God's best choice for us because we are suffering the results of bad choices. But the Lord says that if we repent, He will forgive us and keep us on paths of righteousness to ensure future victories over our enemies. God promises to cleanse us from all our sins and use apparent defeats for our good. Hallelujah!

The decision is up to us as believers. When the Lord commands us to repent and turn from our wicked ways, we need to do just that.

If you feel you have made wrong choices, take this moment simply to repent. Ask the Lord to reveal any leaven and repent for any ungodly multiplication.

List below areas in your life where there is leaven.

1.
2.
3.

Do you recognize patterns of ungodly multiplication, such as lies leading to more lies, lust leading to adultery, or pornography leading to sexual addictions? If yes, list them below.

1.
2.
3.

It Is Alive!

Both positive and negative yeast are active and alive. Is the yeast of sin active and alive in your life right now? Dear ones, there is a more active and higher power!

The Word of God is alive and full of power! It will cut through hidden thoughts and heart issues and expose who we really are.

> For the word of God is full of *living power*. It is sharper than the sharpest knife, cutting deep into our innermost thoughts and desires. It exposes us for what we really are.
>
> Hebrews 4:12, NLT (emphasis mine)

Allow this living power to become alive within your heart and life. Destroy all by repenting for every hidden sin and iniquity, and His Word will be like positive yeast in your life, delivering you from all oppression and yokes of bondage. As a result you will be increased in God. "But the word of God grew and multiplied" (Acts 12:24).

No Leaven = Open Heaven

N ever compromise.

O pen your heart to receive truth at all times.

L eave denial at the Jordan.

E very battle should be devoted to the Lord.

A ccept responsibility for your sins and then repent.

V ow that you will utterly destroy all and keep
your vow.

E ach time of breakthrough, give the glory to God.

N egativity multiplies into more negativity.

Five

The Seducing
Amalekite Spirit

Now go and smite Amalek, and utterly destroy all that they
have, and spare them not; but slay both man and woman,
infant and suckling, ox and sheep, camel and ass.

1 Samuel 15:3

I have lost my anointing! What am I going to do?" Ann
was crying hysterically. "Now when I minister there
is no life in my words. When I sing, the words seem
to fall to the ground. My life is in the anointing, and now
it is gone!"

It was true: God's anointing upon Ann's life was di-
minishing. The pastor's heart was sad. What could he say

at this point? His thoughts went back to three years ago, when he first met her.

Ann came to the ministry for counseling because her life was in shambles. Her lifestyle of sexual perversion and drug abuse had opened doors to uncontrollable mental torment. Because the enemy had such a firm grip on her emotions, she was battling thoughts of suicide.

The first time the pastor saw her walk through the threshold of the church building, he could recognize an anointing upon her life, even through her tormented countenance. It was one of the strongest anointings he had discerned; she was definitely "chosen."

Within a few days she joined the ministry. She stated that she felt the presence of God and knew that she finally had found her place. During her first counseling session the pastor explained to Ann the importance of her commitment to locking into her destiny. He began encouraging her to submit to deliverance and biblical counseling to ensure a strong foundation. Her determination for freedom charted her destiny course.

Two years passed. Ann experienced great levels of deliverance from demonic oppression. Her countenance took on a new "glow," and she developed a beautiful, sparkling smile. She stood straight, holding her head high. The shame of her past had departed. She became one of the ministry's worship leaders, and when she sang the anointing charged the atmosphere. The pastor was so proud of her determination to be free that he gave her responsibilities of leadership.

Then Ann began to go backward. She met a young man whom she declared had "swept her off her feet."

The pastor saw the enemy's strategy from afar and called her for a counseling session. During the hours together they discussed her previous patterns of sexual deviation, bondage and past defilement. With warnings of backsliding, the pastor coached her through lustful temptations that might arise.

"I know, I know," Ann tried to assure him. "You don't need to worry. I will never go back to that lifestyle again. The anointing is too precious to me. Besides, he is a Christian." The pastor knew how many Christians make that very statement only to end up in sexual defilement.

Periodically the pastor would ask Ann to check in with him, just to reassure him that she was still on the right track with the Lord. She would commit to time together and then within a few days cancel the session. She continued in her new relationship, and he remained in prayer for her. He began to notice that Ann was not attending church services. At other times, she would appear through the door of the church to assist in leading worship and then immediately exit from the building. When the pastor approached her concerning her commitment, she shrugged off the responsibility due to her dating schedule. It was apparent that this relationship was more important than her ministry.

The pastor wanted Ann to be happy and find fulfillment in a relationship. He tried to convince her of his concern that she would backslide into sin and not fulfill her destiny. She, on the other hand, disregarded his concern and labeled it all as control. Her entire countenance began to change, along with her attitude.

When Ann did appear to lead worship, the pastor began to notice her lack of anointing. Little by little, the life in her smile and countenance was dying—and worst of all, the anointing diminished almost completely. It reminded him of Saul. Because Saul did not utterly destroy all God had commanded, his entire destiny was aborted.

The pastor made one last attempt to minister to her. "Remember the story of Saul and how God instructed him to smite Amalek? You have got to utterly destroy all. Don't go back to an old lifestyle."

"Yes, Pastor," she rolled her eyes and spoke sarcastically. "I know what you are trying to say, but I am not sleeping with him!" The pastor's discernment spoke loudly, and he was certain she was not telling the truth.

Finally the pastor had to let go and trust God to protect her. He grew increasingly concerned for the worship team because he knew the effects of "a little leaven." Sexual sin on any church team opens the door wide to the enemy.

A few Sundays later the pastor noticed disunity among the entire worship team. They were unable to agree on songs, the sound system could not be perfected, they were disrespectful to the worship leader, and Ann especially was disagreeable. Worship became difficult to press through, and the entire congregation became unable to enter fully into God's presence. It was now obvious. The seducing spirit had gained its entrance, and the congregation was affected. The leaven had multiplied.

How the pastor grieved the morning Ann opened her mouth but could not sing a note! Her voice struggled to find the proper pitch. It was scratchy. Then she forgot her words. In a total panic, she ran off the platform and rushed into the hallway. The pastor followed her and found her crying hysterically.

Ann knew the anointing had diminished and why it had left. "I have lost the anointing, and the anointing is my life!" She began to sob hysterically.

The pastor tried to comfort her. He made many attempts to counsel her. There was no response. The pastor has not seen Ann since that day.

Though these experiences did not actually involve me, they are a true account. I have documented the conversation with permission from a pastor friend. (I changed the woman's name for her protection.)

Even though I was not directly involved, I can identify with this struggle, and sadly I must testify that it is a common story. Though each situation is unique, the stronghold is always the same.

The Amalekite Destiny Thief

The devil is determined to touch the anointed ones of God. Satan, working through the Amalekite stronghold, is pilfering God's anointed saints little by little, strategy by strategy, slowly but steadily stealing our strength and anointing.

"Touch not mine anointed, and do my prophets no harm" (1 Chronicles 16:22). The word *touch* in this passage means "to touch, reach, strike, defeat and be struck by disease." Satan intends to strike against us with methods of wickedness and, if possible, inflict all types of sickness and disease.

It is important to discern which spirit we battle when destiny is aborted. The Amalekite destiny thief is the one Satan assigns to seduce us into wickedness. Under the Amalekite influence we attempt to hold onto the best of what makes us feel good and not completely consecrate our hearts and minds to God. It is the stronghold that encourages us to remain disobedient and continue to embrace sin and compromise. It is responsible for the compromising attitude that states, "I do not have to utterly destroy all. I will not smite my enemy!" Choosing not to utterly destroy aborts destiny.

Saul was seduced by the Amalekite stronghold when it struck him with the wicked seduction of disobedience and pride. Seduction is not limited to sexual perversion, or to disobedience and pride. Seduction involves persuading a person to believe a lie.

The Amalekite stronghold seduced Saul, and subsequently he chose not to smite his enemy. The word *smite* means "to strike, beat, or kill."[1] If we do not slay—kill and utterly destroy—every trace of an Amalekite stronghold, then we will find ourselves backsliding with compromise just as King Saul did.

And just as Ann did. The Amalekite stronghold convinced Ann to compromise her morals and not utterly destroy all the leaven, and this led to a multiplication of sin and rebellion. If we are not careful, the seducing spirit will do the same to us.

By observing Ann's life we can identify the strategies of the Amalekite:

1. The seducing spirit targets a person.
2. The person is seduced, opening the door to the spirit.
3. The person enters into sin.
4. The person gives the enemy a seated position in his or her life.
5. The spirit gains a stronghold.
6. The person begins to backslide.
7. The person begins to compromise.
8. Multiplied defilement occurs.
9. Destiny is aborted.

Let's put two and two together here. When God commands us to "get out the leaven" and to "utterly destroy all," immediately we are tempted to compromise and retain the best part. Oh, yes, we might get rid of a few sins, but most likely we will hold onto the sin we enjoy the most. When there is a strong seduction of compromise, look for the Amalekites! "For if ye live after the flesh, ye shall die: but if ye through the Spirit do mortify the deeds of the body, ye shall live" (Romans 8:13).

The Amalekite Spirit's Methods of Destruction

Saul was only one of many in the Bible whose destiny was stolen through deceit and seduction. The Amalekite stronghold negatively influenced him in different ways. Let's take a look at the methods of destruction that the Amalekite stronghold used against King Saul and still uses against us today.

Method of Destruction # 1: Disobedience

Saul was deceived into disobedience. As he led the attack against the Amalekites, he chose not to utterly destroy all. He feared man more than God.

Saul battled the spirit of the Amalekites and therefore could not utterly destroy them. That in itself tells us that when we battle an Amalekite stronghold, a spirit of compromise, disobedience and rebellion attacks us. That defiling spirit wears us down so we cannot utterly destroy what God has commanded. We easily find ourselves as Saul—rebellious, stubborn and in denial of our sins.

Let's look once again at 1 Samuel 15 and very carefully observe the events that took place in Saul's life so that we can discern how the Amalekite spirit operates. Saul was instructed to:

1. Smite Amalek.
2. Utterly destroy all that they had.
3. Spare them not.
4. Slay both man and woman, infant and suckling, ox and sheep, camel and donkey.

Now let's review Saul's response to God's instructions:

1. Saul took Agag, the king of the Amalekites, alive and destroyed all the people.
2. He spared the best of the sheep and oxen, the fatlings and the lambs and all that was good.
3. He would not utterly destroy them.

Saul gave reasons for his disobedience:

1. "The people made me do it!" He denied his sin.
2. He feared the people and obeyed their voice.

Since Saul was battling the Amalekites during his disobedience, we can discern that the spirit among the Amalekites seduced Saul into areas of disobedience. The Amalekite spirit that prevailed in the city was strong enough to seduce the king of Israel into denial of his actions and rebellion against God's commandments. Saul made a covenant with this ungodly spirit, and as a result he moved into disobedience.

Just as the devil convinced Saul that he did not have to "utterly destroy all," he convinces us of the same—if we are not alert! Just as the Israelites wanted to return to the leeks and garlic of Egypt (see Numbers 11:4–6), we are tempted to go back into defilement. We want to hold onto previous patterns of sin and behavior. If we allow it, the Amalekite stronghold convinces us that we do not have to change in order to move forward with God's Spirit.

But the Lord is requiring obedience from today's leaders. We can no longer fear man or remain in religious tradition. When we embrace more of His Spirit, God requires us to let go of the old. Old behavior, old thought patterns and the traditions of man must be sanctified and tried with His holy fire.

Saul lacked an important key needed for God's blessing: obedience. Our obedience to God's Word releases blessings upon our lives. Let us seek His blessing by obeying His Word to us.

Method of Destruction #2: Rebellion

Saul rebelled against the instructions of God—he chose to do the opposite of what God said. Rebellion is disobedience, but it is also opposition and defiance to the one in authority.

Saul chose to defy God's commandments, and therefore the prophet Samuel brought correction. In the Word of the Lord brought by the prophet, God proclaimed His displeasure of the king and removed the kingdom from Saul.

When a leader is disobedient and in rebellion, his or her offspring of spiritual reproduction eventually will be the same. A leader who has fruits of rebellion will have a congregation in rebellion.

This is the spiritual principle of sowing and reaping:

> Be not deceived; God is not mocked: for whatsoever a man soweth, that shall he also reap. For he that soweth to his flesh shall of the flesh reap corruption; but he that soweth to the Spirit shall of the Spirit reap life everlasting. And let us not be weary in well doing: for in due season we shall reap, if we faint not.
>
> Galatians 6:7–9 (see also Job 4:8; Hosea 10:2)

Method of Destruction #3: Lack of Repentance

Saul did not repent for his disobedience, for true repentance brings change. Instead, bitterness and resentment built within Saul's heart. He did not take personal responsibility for his choices of disobedience but blamed "the people":

> And Samuel said, Hath the LORD as great delight in burnt offerings and sacrifices, as in obeying the voice of the LORD? Behold, to obey is better than sacrifice, and to hearken than the fat of rams. For rebellion is as the sin of witchcraft, and stubbornness is as iniquity and idolatry. Because thou hast rejected the word of the LORD, he hath also rejected thee from being king. And Saul said unto Samuel, I have sinned: for I have transgressed the commandment of the LORD, and thy words: because I feared the people, and obeyed their voice.
>
> 1 Samuel 15:22–24

Today there is much revelation concerning repentance. In fact, repentance has become a major move of God's Spirit.

Strategic prayer revivals are held in convention centers where national prayer leaders call for corporate repentance. Prayer warriors are repenting for city and national governments. Leaders are repenting for the sins against Native Americans and other minorities. This has brought healing to the nation.

An Amalekite stronghold fights against repentance. It reinforces shame and blame, which hinder us from taking responsibility for our own actions. It also reinforces codependency (needing approval of others) and control issues. We see these sins exhibited in Saul's behavior; he blamed others for his actions, wanted the people's approval and took matters into his own hands (control).

Saints must always remain teachable and accountable. We also should strive to reach mature levels of trusting God and His ability to build His Church. Control issues need to be recognized, repented of and then laid at the cross. Only then can we embrace fully the new place God has for each of us.

Method of Destruction #4: Witchcraft

Have you noticed King Saul's bad attitude? He was prideful, rebellious and stubborn. God was so upset with him that He said his attitude and rebellion were equal to witchcraft and idolatry!

> For *rebellion* is as the sin of *witchcraft*, and *stubbornness* is as iniquity and *idolatry*. Because thou hast rejected the word of the LORD, he hath also rejected thee from being king.
>
> 1 Samuel 15:23 (emphasis mine)

By examining this passage, we can identify the strategy of the Amalekite destiny thief. A stronghold was in operation when Saul battled the Amalekites. The demonic influence from the Amalekites infected and influenced Saul's own

life and motives. The same spirit that affected the Amalekites also began to affect Saul, therefore influencing him to
become rebellious and stubborn. As a result, God equated
this sin with witchcraft.

When we hear the term *witchcraft*, we most often envision an ugly old woman with a crooked nose and warts
dressed in black, creating an evil brew in a big pot and
riding around on a broom. But witchcraft is much more
than a fairy tale. Witchcraft is very real, and it is a demonic
system that gains power through control and manipulation, seducing people into rebellion and stubbornness.
Where there are rebellious hearts there is witchcraft. God
recognized Saul's desire to control and manipulate, and
He called it witchcraft. Saints, just think of this: If we are
disobedient and rebellious, God says we have committed
sins of witchcraft and idolatry!

Caught in the act of disobedience and rebellion, true repentance would have placed God's favor back upon Saul's
life. Scripture does point out that Saul admitted his sin,
but never repented and changed. Knowing the outcome of
Saul's disobedience and rebellion should challenge each of
us to guard our hearts and actions. Being quick to repent
will always bring us nearer to the heart of the Father.

Method of Destruction #5: Fear of Man

In 1 Samuel 13:11, Saul once again blames the people for
his sins of disobedience. He had been instructed to wait for
the prophet Samuel to make the sacrifice to the Lord. Instead of waiting, Saul performed the sacrifice prematurely.
Saul stated that he did so because he "saw that the people
were scattered from me . . . and that the Philistines gathered
themselves together." In other words, he was afraid that if
he did not go ahead and perform the sacrifice—even though
God said not to do so—then the people would leave him.
This is what is referred to as the "fear of man."

People in godly authority are often tempted in the same manner. Pressures come from people who desire their own way. Many saints use intimidation and control to get what they desire. They throw around their power, using their influence to take people out of a church. If leadership succumbs to people-pleasing measures rather than standing in godly authority and doing what is correct, doors are opened to controlling powers of witchcraft within the church.

Saul was more concerned with pleasing people than pleasing the Lord. He had a defiled root system in his life—a root system full of selfishness and self-centeredness that would not submit to the instructions of the Lord. The Word of God says that the fear of man will bring a snare upon us—a snare of disobedience that will lead to our destruction. It is more important to be obedient to the Lord than to operate in the fear of man.

Leaders must always be more concerned with pleasing God than with pleasing man. This does not mean, however, that leaders are to be unaccountable. In fact, an even greater accountability occurs in the hearts of leaders when they do follow God and not man. Remaining open to correction and continuing to be teachable only increases with increased leadership responsibility.

Method of Destruction #6: Loss of Vision

When Saul was first chosen as king, he was fearful. He actually ran from the call. The prophet Samuel anointed him as king, though Saul did not desire the call. When he finally surrendered to be king, God was faithful to pour His favor upon him. Life was good for Saul—until he fought the Amalekites. Suddenly the Amalekite spirit struck out against the leader, and he was seduced into apostasy. The favored king was rebellious and disregarded the Word of the Lord.

In the attempt to take the Amalekites, Saul lost his vision. He knew what he was instructed to do. He could taste the victory and see the dedicated spoils given to the Lord, yet he was seduced into rebellion and disobedience. No longer could he see the prize of obedience. No longer was obedience enough. Fame, fortune and individual selfish victory overrode his godly vision.

The Scripture says that when there is no vision, the people perish (see Proverbs 29:18). When Saul lost vision he began to die. Death was pronounced over his kingship, and he became tormented and anguished for the rest of his life.

Is it like that with us at times? We go through life wanting to be used by the Lord, knowing that we have a destiny. Then God calls us, and suddenly we feel inadequate and try to run. Then we finally submit to the call and go into battle against the enemy of our soul. Suddenly we are faced with an Amalekite spirit that seduces us into sin, and we are back where we started.

Within each of us is a God-given vision. When destiny is stolen, vision is stolen. When we lose vision we often feel as if we are dead. But if we repent, the Lord will be faithful to resurrect what seemed to be dead.

Many times I have felt that I have lost vision—especially when I am going through an extreme demonic attack. I want to quit and throw in the towel. So many times I have been tempted to run away from my calling. Numerous times I have lost hope, and it seemed as if nothing God said was coming to pass. In many of those seasons, the Lord told me that it was death to season and not death to vision. When we feel dry and desolate, it may be simply a death to the season and not time for the vision to come to pass.

Sometimes, do you feel as I do—that you take one step forward and then two steps back? There is an Amalekite attempting to steal your vision and your destiny. God is not a liar. What He has promised He will surely do! Don't stop now. Repent and start again. Hang in there and fight for your promise!

Take a few moments and repent of:

- Control
- Manipulation
- Pride
- Rebellion
- Disobedience
- Agreeing with Satan's lies
- Lack of submission
- Illegitimate authority
- The fear of man

Ask the Lord to renew your vision and empower you to fulfill destiny.

Characteristics of the Amalekite

We have revealed the methods of destruction used by the Amalekite stronghold to seduce us into wickedness. Now let's look at some other characteristics of the Amalekite stronghold.

The Amalekite Is a Strong Territorial Spirit

Different idols are worshiped in different regions, and each idol has a demon behind it. Each demon is empowered to negatively affect our lives and minds. Scripture speaks of the demons behind the idols, meaning that where there is idolatry, there are demons.

Since the Amalekites worshiped idols, much demonic activity was associated with them. When Saul battled the Amalekites, the same spirit that caused the Amalekites to be ungodly and defiled attempted to enlist Saul to its side. The demonic spirits controlling the Amalekites influenced Saul when he began to possess the land. Saul probably was attempting to be obedient to God. He at least thought about destroying all, but he became defiled in his actions as the Amalekites seduced him.

A study of spiritual warfare reveals that territorial spirits in certain areas and cities are satanically designed and intended to seduce and adversely affect the inhabitants of those areas—and can have so much power over a region that they can even influence visitors. When Paul went to Corinth, for example, he was influenced by the spirits that operated within that city. The demonic seat was due to the extreme idol worship in the territory.

The same happens to us today as we travel into different states and regions. Whatever spirit is seated in that territory will attempt to pervert God's perfect will for our lives.

Visiting areas of New Orleans, for instance, where there is a great deal of voodoo practiced, can bring strong witchcraft assignments against people. Many have reported being attacked by spirits of infirmity and mind-binding spirits after being in New Orleans. Personally, I have driven into the city and discerned the spiritual darkness in operation.

When an Amalekite spirit is attacking today's churches and leaders, we, like Saul, are tempted to be rebellious, disobedient, prideful and in denial of our sins. This lying spirit of compromise and rebellion has seduced even our cities and regions. We must be aware of the territorial nature of the Amalekite stronghold and guard against it.

The Amalekite Preys upon Our Weaknesses

Throughout biblical history the Amalekites were well-known for preying upon the weak and feeble. This evil confederacy would remain alert, equipped and prepared to assault individuals or straggling families who slowly and feebly lagged behind a transient camp. Their tactics were either to kill the stragglers and take the spoils, or to seize them as slaves. So when the Israelites were wandering in the wilderness, the cloud of glory guided them by day and the pillar of fire during the night. But if any weak and feeble were moving too slowly, the Amalekites would move in for the kill.

This is still true of the Amalekite spirit today. When we attempt to gain victory over strongholds in our lives, we also have contact with powers of darkness. The enemy waits for any opportune moment to catch us in our points of weakness and steal our birthrights by seducing us into apostasy. He waits until our flesh is weak and then entices us to sin and seduces us to "sell out" our inheritance.

Have you realized, for example, that when you attempt to fast you come up against a spirit that tries to convince you fasting is not necessary? The voice of the evil spirit may sound something like this:

Don't you know that fasting is Old Testament?
Jesus never commanded His disciples to fast.
Fasting is dangerous; you could die from starvation!
Fasting is legalism.

Or when you attempt a fast, every minute of your day is consumed with thoughts of cake, ice cream and multitudes of sugar-laden delicacies. Fleshly cravings are part of it, but also demons are at work tempting you to quit your fast. Remember, Satan tempted Jesus while He was fasting. Most likely he will tempt you as well.

Maybe the enemy is not tempting you with fleshly desires, but the Lord is speaking to you concerning the renewing of your mind. In an attempt to gain victory over impure thoughts, every demon in hell will whisper ugly, defiling thoughts to your mind. The demons swarm from the woodwork when you are cleansing your mind. Quite possibly you will battle, day after day, unclean spirits that will attempt to seduce you into old behaviors.

The Amalekite stronghold preys upon our weaknesses, so we must remain strong and on the alert. We must be ready for the attack of our enemy.

The Amalekite Wants Us to Be Cursed

God specifically told Israel that they were not to take certain spoils from battle, for if they did a curse would come upon them. Saul took items that he was instructed to destroy. We call these "accursed things"—items cursed by God. The Amalekite spirit lures us into taking the accursed things—beliefs, items or wickedness that God has cursed. When we take these things into our lives, then we ourselves become cursed.

Deuteronomy 28 is what many ministers refer to as "The Chapter of Blessings and Curses." In that chapter of the Bible, the Lord lists 21 blessings that result from obedience. Also listed, however, are fifteen curses upon children and material prosperity and more than fifty curses of sickness, crop failures, war, captivity, business failure, defeat, persecution and insanity. The fruits of obedience are fruitfulness in every area, and the fruits of disobedience are barrenness. Barrenness means that there is no fruit, no conception of God's Word and little hope for the future. If we allow the enemy to seduce us into rebellion and stubbornness, then we reap barrenness and curses. Our destinies will be lost.

To put it simply, we are blessed by God if we obey Him and cursed if we choose to disobey. If God speaks to us and commands that we are to utterly destroy all, then we are not to embrace an old sinful nature. Instead we are to utterly destroy every area in our lives that is displeasing to God.

Saul's destiny of happiness, life and victory was cursed and aborted due to his disobedience. We can just as easily be seduced by the Amalekite stronghold into the same compromise if we are not spiritually alert.

The Amalekite Seduces Us into Doubting God

The devil is a liar and a deceiver. John 8:44 says that he is the father of all lies. Satan worked through the Amalekites, a tribe rooted in idolatry, and seduced Saul to spare what was commanded for destruction. The devil does the same with us. So often he speaks into our ears with a sly, seductive voice. The voice may say:

- "You don't have to stop that sin. God loves you. You are under grace and not the law. If you continue to sin, God will forgive you."
- "You don't need to tithe; God does not need your money. Besides, tithing is Old Testament. God does not expect you to tithe in today's Church."
- "You don't need to heed the Word of the Lord. After all, even if you sin, God will forgive you."
- "Did God really say that? It was probably your imagination or a false prophecy."

Saul decided himself what should be spared. But don't you know that once Saul set his feet on Amalekite territory, the devil immediately bombarded his mind, challenging him to negate the Word of the Lord? He convinced Saul that God did not mean to destroy everything; surely he could save the best, right? In other words, Satan, through the Amalekite stronghold, convinced Saul—as he does with us at times—that God really did not know what was best.

"Hath God said?" It has been a question that the enemy has used since the beginning of time. As soon as Adam and

Eve were created, the serpent in the garden came up with the original phrase: "Hath God (really) said?" Satan asked that of Eve, and he is still asking it today: "Did God really say that? Do you really believe you can be healed? Do you really believe God wants you to prosper?" Have you heard that voice before? The devil would like to seduce all of us into doubting what God has said.

The Amalekite Seduces with Money

Did you know that money is neutral? Money has no power. But money becomes evil when the spirit of mammon affects how we use our money and how we view the power of money.

In the book of Joshua, we read about a man who listened to this spirit. After the battle for Jericho, God declared that all the spoils of that city were to be devoted to Him. Achan, however, decided to take some of those devoted things and hide them in his tent. As a result, a curse came upon the entire army of Israel, which resulted in the military defeat at Ai. Joshua sought the Lord as to the reason for the defeat, and God revealed that there was sin in the camp. One person, an Israelite, had taken spoils for himself.

When Joshua confronted Achan, he confessed his sin:

> And Achan answered Joshua, and said, Indeed I have sinned against the Lord God of Israel, and thus and thus have I done: when I saw among the spoils a goodly Babylonish garment, and two hundred shekels of silver, and a wedge of gold of fifty shekels weight, then I coveted them, and took them; and, behold, they are hid in the earth in the midst of my tent, and the silver under it.
>
> Joshua 7:20–21

Achan paid an extremely high penalty for his disobedience. Israel stoned him to death and then burned him, thus purging the nation of the negative leaven in its midst. Yet it was through his own lustful desires that he took things that God had instructed to leave alone.

The Amalekite stronghold seduces with money. When the Amalekite spirit is influencing a city, greed and power are at an accelerated high. Drugs and crime are at peak performance because of the money made in illegal exchanges. When people take money from illegal sources, it is the same sin that Achan committed when he took the accursed things. This type of behavior results in a curse over the entire city, until the curse is broken through prayers of repentance and intercession.

Touch Not the Unclean Thing

At times God demands that we leave certain things alone. For instance, God instructed His children to "touch not the unclean thing":

> Moreover the soul that shall touch any unclean thing, as the uncleanness of man, or any unclean beast, or any abominable unclean thing, and eat of the flesh of the sacrifice of peace offerings, which pertain unto the LORD, even that soul shall be cut off from his people.
>
> Leviticus 7:21

When the phrase *unclean thing* is translated from Hebrew, it means "polluted, defiled and impure." It also translates as "to be defiled by idolatry" or "defiled sexually."

God always had a good reason for commanding that the Israelites "touch not the unclean thing." The Lord foresaw, for example, that the Israelites would be tempted to intermarry with unbelievers and that this would result in spiritual defilement. God foresaw that the Israelites would make ungodly covenants (sexual relations) with the heathen women and eventually be seduced to worship their false gods, thus being defiled with the sin of idolatry. God warned Israel numerous times against intermarriage with nonbelievers because they were seduced so easily into the sins of idolatry.

This is why the Lord so often demanded that Israel was to utterly destroy all whenever they took a city. Saul was warned specifically not to take anything the Amalekites possessed; Joshua gave the same instructions to his army in Canaan. In fact, throughout Scripture we find passages where God commanded His army to utterly destroy all and to touch not the unclean things. And it was always for their own good.

Whenever we allow defilement and refuse to put sin under our feet and keep it there, the sin eventually rises up against us. Its aim is for our total defeat. As I pointed out before, Jesus said that a little leaven leavens the entire lump. Another way to say it is if we ask the devil to dinner, he will bring his suitcase. The devil wants to move in and stay! We are instructed to separate ourselves from sin and the worldly pleasures that attempt to seduce us into ungodly behavior.

> Wherefore come out from among them, and be ye separate, saith the Lord, and touch not the unclean thing; and I will receive you, and will be a Father unto you, and ye shall be my sons and daughters, saith the Lord Almighty.
>
> 2 Corinthians 6:17–18

Utterly Destroy the Amalekites!

Utterly destroy all! This was God's instruction to Joshua and the Israelites. Achan, however, "saw," "coveted" and "took" and thus brought a curse upon the entire tribe of Israel.

109

Many years later, the Lord said the very same thing to Saul. Saul was commanded to separate himself from the lusts of his own flesh. But Saul "saw" and "took" of the best. When Saul disobeyed by not utterly destroying all the Amalekites, Israel was destined to continue fighting them for years to come.

Our fulfillment of God's planned destiny always affects others; it affects generations to come. If we do not utterly destroy all, then our future generations must battle the same strongholds—sometimes at greater intensity.

If Achan had been obedient and not taken the spoils, then Israel would not have been cursed and would not have suffered defeat in the battle at Ai. And Achan and his family would not have lost their lives. If Saul had been obedient and destroyed the Amalekites, Israel would have been spared many future battles. Because they did not utterly destroy all, the Lord proclaimed that Israel would continually be at war with the Amalekites: "The LORD hath sworn that the LORD will have war with Amalek from generation to generation" (Exodus 17:16). The Amalekites thereafter continually rose up against Israel and became one of their worst enemies.

The same holds true with every one of us as believers. When we are not determined to destroy sin, then eventually every area of sin that is allowed to remain rises up to defeat us over and over. And our children suffer.

The spiritual dynamics are the same in every church. We are called out of darkness and into His marvelous light. The commandment to walk in the light of Christ is given to every believer, leader and potential leader. We all are to be separated unto Him, walking in purity and holiness and touching not the unclean things.

Utterly destroy the Amalekites that are among you, saints, and choose to move forward into destiny!

Six

Aaron and Hur, Where Are You?

> But Moses' hands were heavy; and they took a stone, and put it under him, and he sat thereon; and Aaron and Hur stayed up his hands, the one on the one side, and the other on the other side; and his hands were steady until the going down of the sun.
>
> Exodus 17:12

The service was energized with God's presence. Some saints were on their faces, worshiping the Lord. Others were beginning to gather at the altar and embrace each other in love. The worship leader was caught away in a place of glory, strumming his guitar and releasing the sounds of God's presence.

I turned to my husband, Mickey. "This is wonderful," I whispered. "God's presence is so strong. Don't you love the faithfulness of God?"

A loud noise rang through my ears, arresting my attention.

A man seemed to be screaming and yet at the same time weeping uncontrollably. At first I thought it was the result of being in God's presence, and that the Lord was healing the man's heart and at the same time delivering him of some oppressive spirit. But I quickly realized it was the pastor of the church, and I discerned that something was terribly wrong with him. My heart became heavy with a desire to minister life to him. I pondered over what to do. I heard the Lord say, *Go over and encourage the pastor; his leaders have left him. He is very wounded and needs encouragement.*

I told my husband what the Lord spoke to me, and we both left our seats immediately and went to minister to the pastor. As we embraced him, he wept so uncontrollably that he fell to the floor. The Lord spoke to me that the pastor was emotionally and physically exhausted. He had been in a great spiritual battle. His leaders had abandoned him and his wife. Now he was extremely discouraged and weak. Mickey and I began to pray over him, and soon he was able to stand and walk to his office.

We followed him down the corridors to his private office. Shutting the door behind him, he wept even more. Mickey and I became more concerned and offered to continue to pray for him. The pastor made his way to his desk. He sat, cupped his face into his hands and sobbed uncontrollably once more. "I cannot go on; I just cannot take another step! I have no one left to hold up my arms. If I don't have help, I cannot keep going."

My heart sank. I knew well the effect of the Amalekite stronghold, for it is the spirit that attacks the "Aarons" and "Hurs." We had often felt as if we were in the same place as this pastor. I began to recall my own spiritual battles— times when I felt that I had no strength to remain in the race and fulfill destiny. Many times we felt as this man of God did—betrayed, helpless, suffering from loss of vision, with few dedicated people to hold up our arms and serve. *God*, I cried out within myself, *help me encourage this pastor to remain in the race!*

We tried to encourage him. We prayed with him. We counseled him. One thing was certain: He needed real bodies to help him!

When I travel to other churches, it seems as if I hear the same complaint from senior leaders: "There are not enough servants in the house of God." As a result, only a few carry the entire load. I have realized that this is no coincidence, but rather a well-planned strategy of Satan to wear out the saints. The strategy of destroying the Aarons and Hurs, those who hold up the arms of the leaders, began with Moses and his battle with the Amalekites.

Aaron and Hur

Most of you remember that Aaron was Moses' brother and Israel's first high priest. In Exodus 17 we read a particular story about Aaron and Moses and a man named Hur. The story begins in verse 8, where the Amalekites came to fight Israel at Rephidim. Moses then told Joshua to lead the men into battle the next day and said that he, Moses, would stand on top of the hill overlooking the battle with the staff of God in his hand. Joshua did as Moses told him, while Moses, Aaron and Hur went up to the top of the hill. The Scripture says that as long as Moses held up his hand (holding the rod), Israel prevailed against Amalek. But when Moses let down his hand, Amalek prevailed:

> And it came to pass, when Moses held up his hand, that Israel prevailed: and when he let down his hand, Amalek prevailed. But Moses' hands were heavy; and they took a stone, and put it under him, and he sat thereon; and Aaron and Hur stayed up his hands, the one on the one side, and the other on the other side; and his hands were steady until

the going down of the sun. And Joshua discomfited Amalek and his people with the edge of the sword.

Exodus 17:11–13

Moses eventually grew tired during the battle, and his arm muscles waxed weary. Can't you picture it? Moses is desperately attempting to hold up the rod, his muscles beginning to flinch, possibly spasm, tempting him to let down the rod. Moses is thinking, *Spasm, spasm! Hey, guys, can't you see? SPASM!* So Aaron and Hur step in to support their leader. They took a stone and placed it under Moses for him to sit, and they held up his hands, one on each side. They committed to do this until the end of the day.

Because of the servanthood of these two devoted men, Israel gained a victory over Amalek. Aaron and Hur were committed to defeating their enemy and, therefore, were empowered to make an even stronger commitment to their leader. Since both of them had been in bondage while slaves in Egypt, no wonder they desired total victory over every enemy. I am certain that their arms grew just as weary as Moses', yet their determination to achieve destiny in the Promised Land must have given them supernatural strength to remain in their position of servanthood.

 Israel won as the result of awesome teamwork—Moses with Aaron and Hur, and Joshua commanding the troops. No victory is substantial without teamwork. We need each other. An effective army learns to fight together and remain together.

During the battle the Amalekites observed what happened when Aaron and Hur held up Moses' hands. Eventually they caught onto the battle plan. In fact, if they could have shot arrows to destroy Aaron and Hur, they probably would have! They would have aimed at Moses, too, I am sure.

It is interesting to note that this battle was in the area of *Rephidim*, which means "to support" (as holding up from the bottom).[1] It was vital to the success of Israel that Moses had those men to support him. In the same way today, it is vital that church leaders have modern-day Aarons and Hurs to support them in ministry. The leaders cannot do it all themselves. If every saint in the kingdom of God fully understood the principles of servanthood, there would be continual victory in the house of God.

But once again, we face an enemy. Satan knows that he can weaken every leader if there is no one to hold up that leader's arms. Because of the importance of the Aarons and Hurs in the Church, the Amalekite stronghold will attempt to win many battles by removing them. The Amalekite spirit deceives God's children into believing that their positions of servanthood are unimportant and menial, and it is therefore difficult to keep servants motivated.

While we served as pastors of a local church, I observed too often how the enemy would constantly attack our Aarons and Hurs. Our pastoral team and our team of leaders were chosen by God to support us and hold up our arms. We would not have been able to press into our destiny if not for the commitment of those who supported us in our local assembly. I have thanked the Lord over and over for so many of our precious leaders and saints who committed to support us and stand with us, especially in times of great adversity.

Dear ones, if you are an Aaron and a Hur to your leaders, God bless you! The work of the Lord could not be possible without *your* commitment and dedication to the plans and purposes of God.

The Amalekites' Special Target: Aaron and Hur

As I mentioned, the Amalekite spirit especially targets the Aarons and Hurs in the Church. This destiny thief spins its web of wickedness seeking to ensnare chosen leaders, so that it can then devour all God's chosen people. The devil recognizes that if he can remove God's chosen from destined authority, then the victory is his. Any military officer is aware that if you are able to remove the head, the body dies. This is why Satan targets those in leadership positions.

Thinking in the natural, when the head is sick, the entire body suffers. Have you ever experienced a migraine headache? You cannot think, function or make quality decisions if the head hurts. If Satan can attack the head, the body cannot fully function.

The Amalekite spirit dictates our pace of growth and attempts to abort destiny by targeting the Aarons and Hurs in the Church. This stronghold targets personal destiny so that the spirit can affect corporate destiny and breakthrough.

We Must Stay Strong

In the last chapter we saw that the Amalekites were notorious for preying upon the weak and feeble. And we saw that today Satan uses the same warfare tactics against us as he did in King Saul's day. As Aarons and Hurs in the Church, we must be acutely aware of this tactic of the enemy.

Sometimes he persuades Christians to remain weak Christians. They choose spiritual immaturity over growth; they are feeble in their walk with God. They lag behind with their negativity, doubt and unbelief. And Satan targets those among God's people who labor endlessly, caring for the flock, and who have become exceedingly weary and feeble—and consequently are moving slowly out of sheer exhaustion. They have no strength to fight, which makes them easy prey. The enemy lingers in the darkness, waiting until the right moment. Then when they are separated from the camp, he authorizes destruction. To ensure a victory, he has executed a well-planned strategy to weaken us. Satan is committed to his task and very seldom backs off easily. He does his job well, for his purpose is to speak out against the purposes of God (speaking lies to us) and to wear out the saints of God.

> And he shall speak great words against the most High, and shall wear out the saints of the most High, and think to change times and laws: and they shall be given into his hand until a time and times and the dividing of time.
>
> Daniel 7:25

We must be alert, Aarons and Hurs! We must not allow ourselves to become weary and feeble. We must not lag behind, or we become easy prey for our enemy. We must remain strong in the Lord, calling on the power of His might, in order to push forward into destiny.

Sickness and Wickedness

The word *Amalekite* is a Hebrew word. It is a derivative of a root word meaning "incurable sickness" and "desperately wicked."[2] This spirit will attempt to do exactly as its name states—continually attack with wickedness, sickness and disease. These are some of the strongest ways the Amalekite spirit attacks the Aarons and Hurs in the Church.

The Amalekite spirit captivates through diseases, mental torment and mental illnesses. We see this spirit active in hospitals, where people are afflicted with all kinds of diseases. But the spirit also seeks to attack with spiritual sickness; Satan has assigned spirits of wickedness to hold us captive in defiled, polluted behavior.

Spiritual wickedness is at its peak when the enemy can seduce us into believing his lies. He wants to seduce us, for

117

example, into believing the lie that we cannot be healed—or that God's will is for us to remain sick! There are many Scriptures that declare God's divine will to heal us. God Himself declares that He is our healer (see Exodus 15:26). But the enemy knows that if he can entice the children of God to compromise and agree with his wickedness, then he has gained legal entrance into their lives.

Satan is a cruel taskmaster, and he will attempt to bring much hardship upon God's children. With legal entrance, he can inflict heavy toil, great pain and incurable sickness upon leaders and those destined to be leaders. Where wickedness is at work, Satan's every evil purpose is being fulfilled. If Satan can continue his attacks, which cause us to remain weak and disabled, he will stalk us like a predator to completely devour us.

Keep in mind that the Amalekite stronghold is very sly in its tactics. Satan is a master deceiver, and he will use whatever tactics necessary to wear us out. Then he will lie in wait until we are tired and weary, when the Amalekite spirit will mercilessly attack with illness and disease.

The Amalekite spirit also preys on our weaknesses, areas of our lives where we are most easily tempted—areas that have "strong holds" on us. This spirit promotes wickedness through temptations such as lust, perversion, pornography, disobedience, fear, alcohol, drugs and the partaking of unclean things (through impure thoughts, impure actions or even areas of disobedience).

What has "hold" of you? Dear Aarons and Hurs, in order to hold up the arms of God's leaders, we must tear down the strongholds of the enemy.

Tearing Down Strongholds

A stronghold is anything that holds us captive. The Bible also refers to strongholds as "high places." By carefully examining Ephesians 6:12, we notice that wickedness is seated in a "high place":

> For we wrestle not against flesh and blood, but against principalities, against powers, against the rulers of the darkness of this world, against spiritual wickedness in high places.
>
> Ephesians 6:12

The high things are the things exalted above the character and Word of God—thoughts, belief systems, attitudes, ungodly lifestyles or any area where Christ does not rule and reign. Any time something in our lives is seated in a higher position than Christ, it must be torn down. In the Old Testament, the Lord sought after kings and leaders who would go up and tear down the altars in high places. God still seeks after men and women of God who will not allow Satan to be enthroned in any area of their hearts and lives. We, too, must go up and tear down mind-sets and false belief systems that have been exalted above the knowledge of God.

A stronghold begins in the mind. If we can begin to renew our minds with the Word of God, then we will initiate the tearing down of the fortress, which holds us captive.

> (For the weapons of our warfare are not carnal, but mighty through God to the pulling down of strong holds;) casting down imaginations, and every high thing that exalteth itself against the knowledge of God, and bringing into captivity every thought to the obedience of Christ.
>
> 2 Corinthians 10:4–5

We will not be able to fight against the Amalekite stronghold with carnal weapons; rather, we must fight with faith and the Word of the Lord. We must cast down our imaginations, meaning that we have to tear down old belief systems about ourselves and replace those thoughts with the Word of God. When the enemy attacks your mind and says that you will be barren and never experience the fullness of your promise, cast down that thought and replace it with a bold confession of faith. <u>As a submitted believer, resist the devil and he must flee</u> (see James 4:7)!

If we have committed hearts, remaining obedient and pure in motive, we are less vulnerable to attack. By closing every door of sin, renewing the mind to the perfect will of God and remaining in obedience, the Lord can become our stronghold and high tower. He desires to be our fortress and strength, and He waits for our decisions to make Him Lord of our lives.

Through dedication to His purposes and repentance of past sins, the enemy can be defeated. Where there is repentance, there is always a victory. The enemy cannot overcome us unless we choose to surrender. So stand firm and see God's promises to you fulfilled! Satan's goal is for you to concede and submit to his temptations of wickedness, but with God's authority you can rise above every circumstance and soar like an eagle.

Don't Sell Your Birthright

The Amalekite spirit also tries to tempt Aarons and Hurs to sell their birthrights. In this way, it persuades us to abort destiny.

The Amalekites were descendants of Esau, the brother of Jacob who sold his entire inheritance for a bowl of soup. He lost everything he had been given because of a temporary fleshly desire. Because Esau chose not to consider the value of his godly inheritance, God chose not to honor Esau. In fact, God was so upset about this that He declared himself as God of Abraham, Isaac and Jacob—not even mentioning being the God of Esau, who should have been the one to be named because of his birth order!

Esau's lack of self-discipline canceled his spiritual destiny in God. What does this speak today to each of us? This is what happens to our destiny when we allow the flesh supremacy. When the Amalekite spirit is in operation, our flesh is magnified. If our flesh is in an exalted place of authority, then we become heavily tempted with worldly desires, and we easily sell out to the world. The enemy comes at our weakest moments and then seduces us to trade our purity and godliness for sinful worldly pleasures. We forfeit our leadership callings and spiritual passion, we forfeit our marriages, we forfeit the benefits of our inheritance, and we forfeit destiny.

Our birthright as children of God promises an inheritance. But if we choose to be children of Belial, our inheritance is canceled and there is no fulfillment of promise.

We cannot, under any condition or circumstance, sell our birthright! No matter what fleshly desire attempts to seduce us, we must maintain our position of godly inheritance.

Don't sell your birthright!

The Planting of the Lord

The Amalekites had a history of being a wandering tribe with no sense of permanence. As a result, they had no respect for covenant relationships among themselves or with anyone else. Having no commitment to each other, they were self-indulgent and self-centered. They inherited from Esau the need for instant gratification and immediate satisfaction, rather than the fruits of patience, long-suffering and peace. Just as Esau disregarded the covenant he had with God, many of his descendants did the same. As a result of being a non-covenantal people, the descendants of Esau became enemies of God and continually battled against the Israelites generation after generation.

Also as a result of not being a covenant people, they eventually became idol worshipers. As we have seen in previous chapters, Scripture speaks often concerning the curses upon the generations of those who worship idols. Idolatry is prohibited by the Lord and considered an accursed thing. Remember that where there is idolatry, there is sin and wickedness. When idolatry is a stronghold, it is very difficult for people to commit to servanthood because they are busy with other "things."

When the Amalekite spirit is in operation, many "things" come before God. Rather than being committed to God, His purposes and His Kingdom, people spend their time and attention on such things as sports, entertainment and pleasure. They have little commitment to the future harvest; all focus is on self and selfish gain and ambition. Every*thing* becomes more important than serving in the house of the Lord. Church leaders become focused on building their own kingdoms, rather than building *The Kingdom*.

Without servants it is impossible for the necessary tasks to be completed in God's house. A handful of committed people cannot accomplish the work of needed hundreds. When this ruthless spirit is working in the local church, there is a lack of commitment and church membership. Since the Amalekites were wanderers and were not committed, you will notice a wandering generation of believers moving from church to church, never committing and never joining as members. These wanderers will never become the plantings of the Lord. They never lock into any assembly. They surf through television channels for "pick a pastor" programs. They are "conference addicted"—they travel from one conference to the next. They are unaccountable to anyone for their actions but still consider themselves to be super-spiritual. Spiritual nomads are uncommitted and selfish toward serving in God's house. How sad that so many of God's saints are missing out on a tremendous blessing that comes through the obedience of serving one another.

The Amalekite spirit seeks especially to keep the Aarons and Hurs from being planted. If this deceitful spirit can tempt these leaders into idolatry, stealing their time and commitment away from Kingdom work, and can keep them from supporting their pastors, then the whole church is affected. Destiny after destiny is thwarted.

God desires that we become planted so that we can bear fruit. Have you ever seen a fruit tree that is not planted bear any fruit? It is impossible for this to happen. Every tree must remain planted so that it can receive the nutrients from the soil. Without soil, nutrients, water and sunshine, no fruit tree will prosper. How can we expect to bear fruit if we are never planted in one place long enough for our roots to take hold?

Dear ones, I implore you to take root. Stay focused on building God's Kingdom. Not only will His Kingdom work then be accomplished, but also you will walk into your destiny!

Division, Destruction and Death

Another strategy of the Amalekite stronghold is to create an atmosphere of disunity within the Body of Christ. If Satan can bring disunity—especially among the Aarons and the Hurs—then the enemy can destroy destiny and bring death to vision within a congregation.

The spirit begins by speaking lies within a congregation. The accuser of the brethren works strongly in conjunction with the Amalekite spirit and begins to accuse falsely. Soon strife dictates division; people become wounded, hurt and offended. Eventually the members begin to separate from one another, and each member becomes vulnerable to attack. Since the Amalekites were well known for picking off the stragglers from a camp, we easily understand why this spirit tries to continually cause separation in a body of believers. As soon as a member withdraws from spiritual oversight and covering, the devil moves in immediately for the "hit."

Like a thief, the enemy's purpose is to steal the destiny of a corporate body as well as from an individual. Where churches are speaking truth and prophesying life and destiny, the enemy continually attacks that church body, trying to steal the seed. Revelation 12:4 says that the devourer stands at the time of birthing to steal the child. This is exactly what Satan does today. He attacks the spiritual wombs of God's chosen with death assignments.

> And she being with child cried, travailing in birth, and pained to be delivered. And there appeared another wonder in heaven; and behold a great red dragon, having seven heads and ten horns, and seven crowns upon his heads. And his tail drew the third part of the stars of heaven, and did cast them to the earth: and the dragon stood before the woman which was ready to be delivered, for to devour her child as soon as it was born.
>
> Revelation 12:2–4

Within each of our spiritual wombs are seeds of destiny that have been planted by God. As He has spoken His will, His Word and His way over each of us, seeds have become impregnated within us, waiting for the appointed time to birth (destiny). The enemy stands close by, just waiting for an opportunity to destroy our destinies—every promise, prophetic word and anointed proclamation the Lord has given us. The enemy knows that if he can steal the seed, our hope and our promise, then he has won the battle.

If we know his tactics, then we can thwart his victory. We can retaliate quickly against his planned attacks by confessing our promises, staying in the Word of God and meeting corporately with believers. We also must be committed to travail with every promise until we fully birth

God's plan for our lives. Just as a woman in labor must commit to the full process for the destiny of her child, we also must commit to the process until we experience results.

Aarons and Hurs, be aware that Satan lies in wait to separate, isolate, deceive and then seduce us into areas of sin and apostasy. Be on guard!

Aaron and Hur: It Is Time for a Name Change!

God wants to give you a new name. He desires to rename you according to the destiny that He has planned for you. He wants to remove the curses and restore you to the fruitfulness that is His will for you. The Amalekite spirit, however, does all it can to prevent this name change—especially among those who are Aarons and Hurs, those leaders in the Church who support the pastors.

In biblical times great significance was placed on the giving of names. Often parents would name their children prophetically, meaning they would pronounce a destiny over the child through assigning a name (title). Rachel, for example, while dying during hard labor in the birth of her second son, announced that his name would be *Benoni*, which means "son of my sorrow." It was not a prophetic name of who he was to become but rather a name given out of her personal pain. Jacob, however, the father, renamed him prophetically, declaring that their son's name would be *Benjamin*, which means "son of his right hand." In biblical times when the father placed his right hand on the son, it represented the passing of the family blessing (see Genesis 35:18). Rachel had named him after her own sorrow, but then the father stepped in and proclaimed a greater destiny over the son and pronounced him to be one who was "blessed."

125

Jacob fully understood the importance of a prophetic name. While his own name was not yet changed at the time of Benjamin's birth, Jacob had most likely already received revelation concerning prophetic names. His own name meant "supplanter" and "deceiver." Both were accurate descriptions of the character he prophetically fulfilled in his younger years.

In Jacob's later years, however, when finally he had come to the end of himself and was all alone and facing one of the largest challenges in life, he became determined to change. Years after he had deceived his brother for the birthright, he was confronted with his past. It was time to face his brother from whom he had once stolen and whom he had deceived. Jacob had betrayed his family and, as a thief, ran off with the blessings. Now he found himself alone with God, facing the future with an "old name." Jacob knew he could go no farther without laying hold of his covenant with God. The results of Jacob's determination led to an all-night wrestling match with the angel of the Lord. The final bell of the match announced Jacob's name change from *Jacob* ("supplanter and deceiver") to *Israel* ("prince of God"). The entire event took place at *Jabbok*, which means "empty."[3] When Jacob was finally empty of self, God could then transform him and proclaim destiny over him, and all his descendants who came after him—God's chosen people.

> And Jacob was left alone; and there wrestled a man with him until the breaking of the day. And when he saw that he prevailed not against him, he touched the hollow of his thigh; and the hollow of Jacob's thigh was out of joint, as he wrestled with him. And he said, Let me go, for the day breaketh. And he said, I will not let thee go, except thou bless me. And he said unto him, What is thy name? And he said, Jacob. And he said, *Thy name shall be called no more Jacob, but Israel: for as a prince hast thou power with God and with men, and hast prevailed.* And Jacob asked him, and said, Tell me, I

pray thee, thy name. And he said, Wherefore is it that thou dost ask after my name? And he blessed him there.

Genesis 32:24–29 (emphasis mine)

Abraham's name, too, was changed from *Abram* ("father") to *Abraham* ("father of many nations"). His wife's name was changed from *Sarai* ("princess") to *Sarah* ("noble woman").

> As for me, behold, my *covenant* is with thee, and thou shalt be a father of many nations. Neither shall thy name any more be called Abram, but thy name shall be Abraham; for a father of many nations have I made thee. And I will make thee exceeding *fruitful,* and I will make nations of thee, and kings shall come out of thee.
>
> Genesis 17:4–6 (emphasis mine)

> And God said unto Abraham, As for Sarai thy wife, thou shalt not call her name Sarai, but Sarah shall her name be. And I will *bless* her, and give thee a son also of her: yea, I will *bless* her, and she shall be a mother of nations; kings of people shall be of her.
>
> Genesis 17:15–16 (emphasis mine)

Both Abraham and Sarah moved forth from their places of barrenness into destinies of fruitfulness when God changed their names. When God renamed them, it was a prophetic declaration of destiny and purpose. Not only were they to fulfill God's purposes for their lives through name changes, but also the name changes were the way God blessed them. In each situation where God changed a name, fruitfulness was promised.

Joshua's name was changed as well. In Numbers 13:16 we read, "These are the names of the men which Moses sent to spy out the land. And Moses called Oshea the son of Nun Jehoshua." The name *Jehoshua (Joshua),* or *Yah Shua* in Hebrew, means "God saves." Joshua was mighty in war and was the successor of Moses in the prophetic office. He became, as his name implies, a great savior of God's elect, to take vengeance on the enemies that rose against them, so that he might give Israel its inheritance. Incidentally, his is the same root as the name of our Savior, Jesus.

God changed names in the New Testament as well. Saul (not to be confused with King Saul, whom we have been discussing) was on the road to Damascus, planning to murder Christians there, when the resurrected Jesus appeared to him, changing his name and his life. The name *Saul* means "desired"[4] (implying what God has desired for us to be). God changed his name to *Paul*, which means "small" or "little"[5] (implying humility), and he was born again into a new destiny. How many of us are like Saul? Sometimes God may have to knock us off of our "high horse" (implying pride and arrogance) to change our names into "humility." Like Saul, it may take a road to Damascus experience before we experience a name change, but in the end it will be worth it!

Jesus' disciple Simon experienced a name change. He was the first disciple to declare that Jesus was "the Messiah, the Son of the living God." And Jesus said to him:

> Blessed art thou, Simon Bar-jona. . . . I say also unto thee, That thou art Peter, and upon this rock I will build my church; and the gates of hell shall not prevail against it. And I will give unto thee the keys of the kingdom of heaven: and whatsoever thou shalt bind on earth shall be bound in heaven: and whatsoever thou shalt loose on earth shall be loosed in heaven.
>
> Matthew 16:17–19

His name, *Simon*, was prophetic. It meant "one who hears."[6] Simon heard the Word of the Lord and believed it. And God changed his name to *Peter*, which means "rock."[7]

In order for a *Simon* ("one who hears") to become a *Peter* ("rock"), he or she may have to press into greater revelation to fully understand the benefits of a name change.

But we face an opposing spirit who does not want our names changed. The Amalekite spirit strategizes against the Aarons and Hurs with lies that they will never experience a name change. Satan is a master deceiver and a liar, and he falsely accuses the servants of God, convincing us that we are unworthy and unneeded in the house of God. The enemy does not want us to know and understand that God wants to change our names.

So many of us were given names based on how someone else perceived us. Often we are the brunt of other people's pain and their own inabilities to cope with life. Out of their own emptiness, many parents may have lashed out against their children with names like "stupid," "dumb," "useless," "worthless" and "ridiculous." These are also names that the devil feeds into our minds. Many times the adversary tells us that we are defeated, worthless and failures. Many of us have believed so many lies from the devil that we believe those lies are our names. We receive those names and identify with them.

During times of great sorrow and pain, we often hold onto old names from our past. We continue to wear our "old garments," which reflect past behavior and character, because we have been deceived to believe that these names define who we are. The Amalekite stronghold attempts to seduce us into believing the lie that we are nothing more than worthless, helpless and defeated. The enemy tries continually to discourage us by speaking old names over us. He plans to deceive us into believing that we can never be changed or transformed into Christ's image.

But our heavenly Father steps in and changes our names. If God will come through for those like Jacob (a liar and deceiver) and the New Testament Saul (a murderer), then He will heal our hearts and change our names.

129

He renames us according to our destinies. Though we were once cursed, He promises to restore! The Word says that we are blessed and not cursed, and it cannot be reversed:

> Behold, I have received commandment to bless: and he hath blessed; and I cannot reverse it. He hath not beheld iniquity in Jacob, neither hath he seen perverseness in Israel: the LORD his God is with him, and the shout of a king is among them.
>
> Numbers 23:20–21

The Word over those barren, unfruitful places in our lives is that we will be fruitful and bear much fruit. We have the "shout of the King," and therefore we can stand strong, knowing who we truly are in Christ.

But in order to bear the fruit we must be determined for destiny. We talked about how Aaron and Hur had to remain determined to hold up Moses' arms. I am sure they grew just as weary as Moses, but they found their place in ministry and fulfilled their responsibility. Their determination to achieve destiny in the Promised Land gave them supernatural strength.

And Jacob held on until he received God's blessing. All too often we quit prematurely. Hanging on until you get the victory of becoming a new man is worth the fight; it is worth believing for and wrestling over. We must become like Jacob and declare to the Lord that we will not let go of Him until He blesses us! We, too, can become the blessed of the Lord if we devote ourselves to Him in every way. We might need a good wrestling match with destiny to become more determined, but we can be certain that God desires to bless us.

Like Abram/Abraham, Sarai/Sarah, Jacob/Israel, Oshea/Joshua, Saul/Paul and Simon/Peter, we, too, can experience name changes. Name changes can be expected when we are born again! It is a fulfillment of His covenant with each of us to be "renamed" by the Spirit. God wants us fulfilled, blessed and experiencing purpose and destiny. We can believe for change and transformation along with blessings because He is a God who does not lie and fulfills His covenant with His chosen people!

Saints, as Aarons and Hurs we have the same empowerment available as Jacob. We can wrestle against the old sinful nature and hang onto the promise of the Spirit as God transitions each of us into a new name. God challenges us to lay hold of our covenant promises, which will empower us to fulfill our destinies.

Fight for your promise, and God will change your name!

How to Receive a Name Change

1. Make a decision that it is time to change.
2. Realize that the enemy has lied and that you have believed his lie concerning yourself and others.
3. Repent for believing the lies and for receiving a false name from the enemy.
4. Begin to believe what God says about you.
5. Become determined and know that receiving a new name from God is worth fighting for.
6. Don't let go until you get it!

Make a Bold Confession

The Lord is calling upon you, the Aarons and Hurs, to beware of the Amalekite! Like Aaron and Hur with Moses during the battle with the Amalekites, make a decision now to do whatever it takes to hold up the arms of your leaders.

Remember that you must destroy all that is unclean and fully consecrate your hearts and minds to God so that you can remain obedient. Stay strong in Christ, so that the Amalekite spirit cannot target you when you are weak or sick. Wrestle against your old, sinful nature, and hang onto the promise of the Spirit as God transitions each of you into a new name. Lay hold of your covenant promises, which empower you to fulfill your destiny. Tear down the strongholds of the enemy—those areas where Christ does not rule and reign. Take root and stay planted, so that you can bear fruit. Don't be tempted into idolatry, and remain committed to Kingdom work, so that you can support your pastors. Don't allow any disunity to come among you.

It is time for you, Aarons and Hurs, to make a bold confession against

1. any physical infirmity or weakness, helplessness and loss of vision;
2. compromise, lack of self-discipline and indulgence of the flesh;
3. becoming a spiritual nomad and not being firmly planted;
4. remaining in darkness, where the Amalekite attacks;
5. selling your birthright and compromising your call in God.

Seven

God's Rods of Righteousness

Neither yield ye your members as instruments of unrighteousness unto sin: but yield yourselves unto God, as those that are alive from the dead, and your members as instruments of righteousness unto God.

Romans 6:13

It was Easter Sunday morning. The sun was shining, the flowers were blooming and signs of life were budding forth everywhere. *Such a glorious representation of a new day, this Easter Sunday*, I said to myself as we drove to church.

A little later, during the service, my thoughts were racing. *O Lord, please build Your Church! You died that we might live. Your blood has ensured victory on every side. This is Resurrection Sunday. Lord, resurrect every area in your Church that appears dead.*

It had been a long, dry season. I was desperate for God to move upon our behalf. I needed to experience a fresh touch of His power. Our entire church leadership needed it. The Bible says, "Hope deferred maketh the heart sick" (Proverbs 13:12), and we were finding this to be so true. Weary and experiencing hope deferred, our leaders needed a touch from God's hand.

The verse concerning God building His Church began to rush through my mind.

> And I say also unto thee, That thou art Peter, and upon this rock I will build my church; and the gates of hell shall not prevail against it.
>
> Matthew 16:18

I began to meditate on this Scripture. God said the gates of hell would never prevail against His Church. Why then did it seem as if hell was victorious over our situations? *Lord, I want to be like Peter. I desire to become that rock upon which you can build. Equip me to become stable in every way so that I am a part of building your Church!* I cried out silently in prayer. It was then that I heard the Lord speak clearly the words that changed my mind-set on building His Church.

First of all, the Lord began to minister to me that *He* would build His Church. Though I served as copastor of the congregation, it was His church and not mine. My part was to labor with Him, but even as I did my part, fulfilling my destiny, it was still His Church to build. It was time to release it to Him.

Second, the Lord began to minister concerning the spiritual warfare of the Church. For years I had pictured the Church as a fortress, standing firm and fortified, but in a defensive position, simply defending her boundaries. I envisioned Satan and his demonic forces attacking the Church, aggressively moving forward in an offensive position attempting to destroy the Church. The Lord spoke to me, however, that the Church was not simply standing still but rather was moving forth in an offensive position.

The Church was moving toward the goal of victory, and hell was not going to be able to rise up against the constant force of power from God's Church.

I had been on the defense too long. I had developed a defensive mentality, almost expecting to be accused falsely and blamed for other people's problems. But God reassured me that He was the one in charge of the Church, and He would build it. The Church of God is not on the defense but is actively, aggressively pursuing her enemy!

And third, the Lord said that the Church would need new "rods of authority" in the days ahead. He began to minister to me concerning Moses' famed rod of supernatural influence. Moses would stretch forth his rod, which God had given him, and miracles would occur. The Lord revealed that His believers of today were becoming rods in His hand, and that we were His battle-axes and His weapons of righteousness. He went on to say that the righteousness in which His leaders walk would defeat the enemy, because righteousness is a weapon that defeats the enemy!

> Neither yield ye your members as instruments of unrighteousness unto sin: but yield yourselves unto God, as those that are alive from the dead, and your members as instruments of righteousness unto God.
>
> Romans 6:13

> Thou art my *battle axe and weapons of war*: for with thee will I break in pieces the nations, and with thee will I destroy kingdoms.
>
> Jeremiah 51:20 (emphasis mine)

God began to reveal to me the Amalekite stronghold that comes to discourage us constantly. This spirit always follows the same progression:

135

- It seduces the sheep into sin, which destroys their destiny.
- When their destiny is destroyed, it affects corporate destiny.
- It leaves very few committed leaders to hold up the arms of the pastors.
- It removes generals who cannot then lead the spiritual battles.
- It steals the "rods" of authority promised to us by the Lord.
- It steals vision and causes hope to be deferred.

What the Lord revealed to me that day was that it was time for the leaders to rise up and begin the offensive. We are to release the building of the Church to Him, but we must be healthy and whole and available to Him to use in the building process. We must not simply be dealing with the enemy on the defensive; we must be ready to be used by God to fight on the offensive and aggressively pursue our enemy, putting him beneath our feet!

So how do we do that? By being God's rods of righteousness, leading His people into victory.

God's Rods of Righteousness Today

It had become my season to understand the significance of these new rods of authority. God was showing me that His rods of righteousness today are more than mere staffs; they are a people. God's righteous people are the rods of His authority on the earth. The Lord wants to hold us up as a rod before our enemy. He will say, "Satan, do you see My sheep? They are My rods of authority because they are righteous. And when they stand as My rods of authority before you, you must flee!"

Isn't that an awesome thought? Imagine your church congregation coming to a Red Sea experience. God holds up your pastor and leaders as rods of righteousness before that Red Sea, and a miracle occurs! Satan's plans of destruction are defeated because of righteous leadership.

Let's take this a step further. What about you and your Red Sea? God will do the very same for your situations. He will use you as a rod against every Red Sea, and you can cross over onto dry land. We all are called to be rods of righteousness, and the Lord desires that we all experience victory on every side!

The appointed and chosen supporters to every leader are weapons (rods) in the purposes of God. Moses stretched his rod across the Red Sea to part it and touched it to a rock to bring forth water, but he also had rods of righteousness that held up his arms: Aaron and Hur. Every minister needs an Aaron and a Hur. Moses was very blessed to have two strongly committed leaders to hold up his arms, as well as a Joshua to lead the troops into battle. Our ministers today need that same committed support. And the enemy especially attacks those who are destined to become the Aarons and Hurs to the Moseses in the Church. He knows that if he can seduce the Aarons and Hurs into sin and areas of defilement, then he can steal life from God's Church.

If you are a Moses in any spiritual capacity, God will use you as a rod to part Red Seas and to strike rocks and hard places for water. And if your calling is to be an Aaron or a Hur, then God will use you to be a rod of righteousness to your spiritual Moses. Begin to believe now for the strength to become a rod of righteousness.

Rephidim: The Place of Support

Exodus 17 describes Moses leading the Israelites in the wilderness. The early part of this chapter describes how

his rod brought forth water from a rock at the commandment of the Lord. After the people were refreshed, they
immediately went into battle against Amalek, the king
of the Amalekites. Moses instructed Joshua to choose
men to fight against Amalek, knowing that the next day
he would view the battle from the top of the hill. Moses
was to stand with an outstretched rod to ensure another
victory.

> Then came Amalek, and fought with Israel in Rephidim.
> And Moses said unto Joshua, Choose us out men, and go
> out, fight with Amalek: to morrow I will stand on the top
> of the hill with the rod of God in mine hand.
>
> Exodus 17:8–9

Moses had faith that God would move each time he
stretched out his rod. Time and time again, he would stretch
out the rod by God's command, and through his faith, miracles would occur. He challenged Pharaoh with it, casting
it down to become a serpent and using it to bring forth
multiple plagues on Egypt. He used it to part the Red Sea.
He used it to bring forth water from a silent rock. The rod
became a symbol of stability, breakthrough and wonders.
Now, as part of the battle strategy, Moses would hold up
that same rod to encourage Israel and release another victory, this time against the Amalekites.

Moses also understood the importance of remaining in
a position where people could see him stretch out his rod.
It is the same in the Church today. A congregation needs
to see Moses holding up his rod. The congregation needs
to witness leaders walking in righteousness. They need to
see Aarons and Hurs who are committed to holding up the
arms of Moses. If a congregation does not witness a rod
constantly held high, then the sheep will begin to scatter,
and the Amalekite spirit will have been successful in split-
ting the congregation.

Maybe Moses did not take into account the length of the battle when he volunteered to extend the rod—and keep it there! (How long did Moses actually have to hold up the rod for all Israel to cross over the Red Sea, anyway?) Or maybe Moses knew that God would make a way, as He had done so many times before, to support the rod. At any rate, Moses did not retreat from his original declaration. He was fully determined to keep the rod extended for all Israel to see.

Moses stood at the top of the hill named Rephidim. As long as Moses held up his hands (holding the rod), Israel prevailed. But when Moses' arms began to tire and fall, Amalek would begin to prevail.

Use your imagination and picture yourself watching the scene where Moses is holding up his hands. Israel sees Moses holding his rod. A roar rips through their spirits as they rise up with tremendous vigor and faith in God. They smite the Amalekites on the left and on the right!

Moses then becomes weary; his hands begin to falter. The rod is no longer in sight! Fear grips the hearts of the Israelites. "Where is Moses? Where is the favor of God?" The soldiers begin to waver; their faith weakens while they struggle to see the rod of victory.

The Amalekites also are watching for the rod. They notice Moses' hands fall to his sides, and the rod disappears.

"Now!" The Amalekite general gives the charge. "Now! Go! The battle is ours!" The Amalekites begin to slay the Israelites; the tide begins to turn.

Aaron and Hur rush to Moses to grab his arms, and up goes the rod of authority once more. The Israelites can see it once again. "The Lord is with us! No weapon formed against us will prosper!"

The Israelites needed to see the rod of righteousness in order to be victorious in battle. They needed to see Moses before them, with Aaron and Hur at his sides supporting him. The same is true in the Church today. We need to see our pastors, our leaders, our rods of righteousness go before us. Only then can we prevail over the Amalekite and achieve victory in God's Kingdom.

Purity Begins with God's Leaders

In order to be rods of righteousness within the Church, we must first be righteous. My spiritual father, Bishop Bill Hamon, has preached on this subject many times. Often I have heard him say that if we do not deal with our sin in private, God will begin to shout it from the rooftops. This is frightening, and yet it is happening more and more.

We all can remember television exposure concerning certain Christian leaders. If some had repented and turned from sin, then there would not have been such tremendous exposure and worldwide knowledge of their sin. I believe these times of exposure may have been necessary for the leaders to recognize the fact that God is calling for purity among His leaders. God is sovereignly building His Church. He is laying the axe to every root that is against His will and calling each of us to purity and holiness. He is setting a standard of purity before us and molding us into the image of Christ, and He is beginning with His leaders.

Righteousness is a rod of authority that we will use to defeat our enemy in these last days. We must learn to fight under the right banner in the right season. In order to defeat the defilement of the Amalekite stronghold, we must gather under the correct banner, or standard.

Coming under banners of religion will not ensure a victory. But gathering beneath the banner of God's plans and purposes will always release victory. The Church must recognize her times and seasons. There is a time to fight under the banner of faith, or beneath His banner of prophecy, but at all times and in every season we need to recognize under which banner we are to gather and fight! Knowing this and acting with faith upon it will release a rod of authority for a great victory.

Servants in the Kingdom

We have seen that if leaders do not have help, then there will be no victory, and that robbing God's house of needed servants is therefore one of Satan's strategies. But as servants we also must know and understand our place in the Kingdom work, not seeking after jobs that are not ours, but rather fulfilling the specific work God has given each of us to do.

We are all part of God's army, and we each have a part to play—a destiny to fulfill. One person may be called to be a general, another a private. One may be a senior leader, another a prayer warrior. But not a single one is more important to God than another. It is a matter of delegated authority, and God is the Commander-in-Chief!

Aaron and Hur were just as important as Moses in the battle against Amalek. Their unified effort guaranteed the victory for all Israel.

God called Caleb, the victor who took his mountain, His "servant" (see Numbers 14:24). A servant is one who simply serves. Not concerned about title or position, his only goal is to serve the Lord's purpose.

Aaron and Hur were serving Moses, but more importantly they were serving the cause of God's full plan of destiny for Israel. The battle was bigger than Moses, bigger than Joshua and bigger than Aaron and Hur. The plan was all about the Lord. It is the same today. It is not about us or receiving our victories; it is about Him and establishing His Kingdom on earth.

I believe that we all are called to serve in God's house in one capacity or another. If you are not in leadership now, most likely you are destined to be at some point. If you serve in any capacity, the devil will try and destroy you. Satan does not want you to fulfill your destiny, and he will use whatever tactic he can to deceive and separate you from God's plan.

Don't let him seduce you into trying to fill a role that is not yours to fill. Remain a servant, a rod of righteousness, in the place God has you. Both your destiny and victory will be assured, but most importantly God's plan will not be thwarted.

Satan Attacks the Watchmen on the Walls

Since it is Satan's strategy to dismantle authority within the local assemblies, most likely he will target the support systems. This includes all areas of leadership—pastors, elders, deacons, department heads—as well as servants and intercessors. A big strategy of Satan is to bring disharmony and strife among God's army, because he knows that fighting among the troops assures defeat. A battle inside the camp leaves the most deadly wound.

As a senior pastor I have observed the enemy's tactics for years. One main way he causes strife and discontent is to contaminate the "watchmen on the walls"—the intercessors—with malicious gossip and slander. Prayer warriors who are called to guard the walls of the Church are often seduced into power struggles, rebellion and strife, creating a very infectious wound. Contamination spreads to others as they begin to make phone calls with false accusations, not only to each other as intercessors but also to others in the Body. You may have heard the contaminated voice; it sounds like this:

- "While in prayer, the Lord showed me that there is sin in the camp. Is God saying the same to you? I cannot worship here anymore!"

- "While I was interceding, I heard the Lord say I was supposed to leave the church. I know others are to leave also. Did you hear the same from God? Will you help me alert others that it is time to leave?"
- "Did you know that while in prayer I heard the Lord say He was removing His Spirit from our church?"
- "While in prayer, I saw the name 'Ichabod' written across the altar of the church. I know I can hear from God. We need to alert the other intercessors! Will you help me make the calls and warn others?"

This voice may sound totally innocent, but the motive is very impure. The hidden agenda behind this "concerned intercessor" is to lead others away from godly protection and oversight and to herself/himself. Many church splits are a result of intercessory teams feeling that they are the ones called to "lead" the church with what they see in the Spirit realm, when in fact they are to remain pure in their hearts, pray for the leaders and support them with their prayers.

At the defeat of Ai, the Lord did not go to the intercessors to have them discern the stronghold. God spoke to Joshua and Joshua only—the leader—and He had Joshua deal with the sin in the camp. Intercessors are to pray. While they will discern sin, they are only to pray concerning that sin—and very discreetly. They are not called to judge the sin—that is the Lord's responsibility. God places leaders in position through His delegated authority, and it is not the intercessors' responsibility to lead the sheep.

Rise Up and Take the Gates!

Satan wants to defeat God's servants in the Church. If the devil can keep us in bondage to sin, he will continue to win the battle. He will cause us to doubt God's Word, doubt our destiny, stir up strife and discontent and keep us in unforgiveness. He will study every weakness and then move with intent of captivity.

Remember: We cannot be held captive in darkness, for we are children of the light! But <u>by tolerating darkness through sin, we leave ourselves open to attack. If we remain disobedient and do not utterly destroy all, we may become like King Saul and be seduced into apostasy.</u>

God is sending us wake-up calls. He is searching the hearts of His leaders and laying His axe to the root of every tree that is not bearing fruit. He is exposing every area of sin and opening our eyes to the gates that we have left open to the enemy—those areas in our lives that we have left vulnerable to attack. He is calling on us to take possession of those gates.

With God's help we can begin to take our personal gates. By taking this promised spiritual ground, we will experience personal breakthroughs that will lead to corporate breakthroughs. The revolving doors that have been legal entrances into our lives will be destroyed permanently as we become effective leaders in God's army.

Saints, it is time to rise up and possess the gates of your enemies! God is calling us to repent, turn from all areas of wickedness and put the enemy beneath our feet.

Repent, Get Planted and Fight!

Are you called to be a leader in the house of God? Have you allowed the enemy to deceive you into leaving your post? If so, it is time to get back into the battle and realign with your destiny links!

Repentance will empower you to move forward into destiny. Ask the Lord to forgive you for leaving your assigned position and then recommit your life to His perfect will and destiny for your life. Know where you are to be planted and remain there. Hold up the arms of your leaders and fight the good fight of faith.

To ensure that you walk in continuous victory, it is important to recognize the situation that caused you to leave your post in the first place. Was it disappointment in leaders? Did someone wound you, and as a result you isolated yourself from the Body? Did you go through a divorce? Are you suffering with a stronghold of shame? Be determined to never allow anything to rob your destiny.

List below the reasons your destiny may be hindered.

1.
2.
3.
4.
5.

Write below the ways that you plan to change your situation and get back into the battle.

Stand as Rods of Righteousness!

Saints of God, we must be healthy and whole, pure and righteous, in order to be available to be used by God. We must be ready to go on the offensive and aggressively pursue our enemy. We must not be sidetracked into a job that is not ours, nor should we be seduced into causing disunity among our camp. We are called to rise up, take back the gates and stand as rods of righteousness and victory in God's Church.

I encourage you to make this bold confession right now: *I will take back the gates. I will take my mountain. I will be a rod of righteousness and achieve my destiny. I will stand as a rod of authority, and Satan will flee!*

Eight

A Time Such as This

Thou art come to the kingdom for such a time as this.

Esther 4:14

Just as it was the appointed time for Queen Esther to come forth, it is now an appointed time for the Body of Christ. It is our anointed and appointed season to arise and come to the forefront, moving purposefully into designated places of spiritual authority.

Many theologians have questioned the importance of the book of Esther. Though God is not mentioned throughout the entire book, one can see clearly that the book reveals God's planned strategy to save His chosen people. I am convinced not only that the book is divinely inspired but also that specific warfare strategy is revealed against the "destiny thief"—the Amalekite spirit.

Step by Step

Esther did not suddenly arrive at destiny. The biblical account of Esther describes how she endured much preparation and then opposition as she pursued destiny.

In preparation for marriage, Esther was anointed step by step. It was customary to deeply cleanse, purify and anoint the female body in preparation for her intimate intercession and relationship with her husband. As we discussed in chapter 3, for twelve months Esther was bathed in exotic and expensive oils. The number twelve is symbolic of new government and authority, meaning that this purification process was necessary before Esther could move into her destined authority—to shift her government! She was chosen by God to change decrees of death against her own people. Step after step toward destiny, Esther was prepared, purified and cleansed as the future bride patiently awaited her specific position of authority.

Esther also was purified with myrrh for six months. The number six is symbolic for flesh or for man. We can conclude that Esther was purified and cleansed from all fleshly desires and sinful nature. This was the process of perfection needed to empower her to become a queen who would shift governments and institute godly decrees.

As I mentioned earlier, during her time of preparation Esther did not enjoy lavish, "Calgon-take-me-away" soakings. She was not simply oiled down or sprayed with perfume like today. Rather, the myrrh was scrubbed into her skin to become a part of her—so that she herself became a sweet-smelling fragrance.

The word *anoint* means not only to smear with grease but also "to rub" with oil. Part of the anointing process, then, is the rubbing and scrubbing. Esther's being rubbed and scrubbed with myrrh was extremely significant. Let's look further at this symbolism:

- Myrrh was sacred oil used to anoint the robes of the priesthood. The priests were "set apart" and anointed as servants in God's house. We also are "set apart" and anointed to serve as priests.

- *Myrrh* translates as "bitter." Esther had been adopted by her cousin, Mordecai, as she had no mother or father (see Esther 2:7). If there was any bitterness in Esther's heart due to rejection or abandonment issues, it had to be scrubbed and rubbed out so that she could come forth into her full destiny. We must allow God to cleanse all bitterness of the past from our lives in order for us to become anointed vessels and fulfill destiny.

- Myrrh was used in burial preparation. There must be a death to self and selfish ambition in order to achieve full destiny.

Like Esther, the Body of Christ is being cleansed to ensure a sweet fragrance for the Lord. He wants us to be that pure fragrance—not just a sweet smell that dissipates in a few hours. He rubs us with His hand in a step-by-step process of cleansing until we are released and empowered to rule and reign in spiritual authority. We are purified from all unrighteousness, iniquity and impurity in order to prepare us for the high calling of Christ Jesus—our purpose and destiny. Like Esther, we are called to shift governmental decrees within our families, neighborhoods, areas of business and even nations! We can easily identify with Esther's process of preparation. Day after day we endure God's process, waiting for our specific times of breakthrough and times of fulfillment. As we study the story of Esther, we see that she symbolized the Body of Christ fulfilling destiny—one step at a time.

The Plot of Haman, the Amalekite

When Esther was chosen as queen, immediate opposition rose up against her and her people. The Amalekite stronghold surfaced, this time in an individual. Haman, a favored prince of King Ahasuerus of Persia, was in an authoritative position over all the Jews. Haman was a descendant of Agag, an Amalekite (see Esther 3:1), and Satan used Haman as his pawn to try to abort the destiny of Israel.

All the people, save Mordecai (Esther's cousin), bowed in homage to Haman as he paraded through the city streets. Haman, humiliated and angered by Mordecai's lack of demanded respect, became enraged and immediately devised a scheme to destroy Mordecai and all the Jews.

Haman approached the king of Persia with his demonically inspired idea that all Jews needed to be destroyed. He convinced the king to believe that the Jews were rebellious and did not respect or support the king's authority. Haman told him they were dangerous and would hinder progress and jeopardize his kingly position if they were not destroyed. Haman's webs of deceit were laced with manipulative words. His pride fueled his fury to destroy God's anointed.

> And when Haman saw that Mordecai bowed not, nor did him reverence, then was Haman full of wrath. And he thought scorn to lay hands on Mordecai alone; for they had shewed him the people of Mordecai: wherefore Haman sought to destroy all the Jews that were throughout the whole kingdom of Ahasuerus, even the people of Mordecai.
>
> Esther 3:5–6

The same plot of destruction is assigned to us if we refuse to bow down to the enemy's strategy. Once we take a stand, as Mordecai did, the Amalekite is swift to devise a strategy of destruction.

After Haman convinced King Ahasuerus that the Jews were rebelling against his crown, the king issued a decree to terminate all living Jews, not thinking that Queen Esther also would be destroyed. Quite clearly the king was influenced by the wicked Amalekite spirit to destroy the destiny of God's chosen and anointed. Haman was so determined to destroy the Jews that he actually offered to finance the entire extermination! He was planning to plunder his enemies and take the spoils. Doesn't that exhibit the same tactics of the Amalekites in earlier history?

It had been five hundred years since Israel's first encounter with the Amalekites following Israel's release from Egypt (see Exodus 17:8–16), and the war continued as prophesied. Half a century later, Satan's seed planted earlier through Amalek was resurrected in another generation.

Esther was called forth at an appointed time to intercede for God's people. She had been chosen and prepared, and now was her anointed time of intercession. Her cousin, Mordecai, exposed the plans of destruction, and she determined to approach her husband—an act that was against the law. Esther called for the Israelites to fast on her behalf, and after three days she approached the king with God-given favor. Esther laid down her life for the destiny of her people. Because her heart was pure and she walked in God's favor, the king heard her pleas for safety. Esther's sacrificial attempt saved an entire nation. The Amalekite plans of destruction were exposed, and Haman was hung on the gallows he had previously prepared for Mordecai!

How awesome it is when God turns the tables back upon our enemy. The Lord uses the same weapons the enemy uses against God's chosen and turns them back upon him. God's Word states that all things work together for our good: "And we know that all things work together for good to them that love God, to them who are the called according to his purpose" (Romans 8:28).

The Hamans of Today

Demonically inspired Hamans are operating today through manifestations of pride and arrogance. The Hamans of today attempt to deceive many. They proclaim that they are called by God to be the Aarons and Hurs, but actually they are jealous of authority and plot to destroy godly leaders. They work behind the scenes, secretly but steadily building gallows to hang and spiritually murder authority. They whisper false accusations to others in leadership and deceitfully approach the congregations in attempts to cause disunity. Many Hamans have wealth and use their financial status to control and manipulate, all to gain personal power in the decision processes.

These spirits also reinforce and protect old structures of religion. Religion is a form and structure of beliefs and practices; it is not relationship and never will be. Simply having a form of beliefs does not replace a true relationship. The present-day Church is being challenged to move past religious mind-sets and pursue God's Spirit. Destiny cannot be accomplished without change, for we are forever being changed (transformed) into God's image.

When I think of Haman I am reminded of Adolf Hitler, who also attempted to annihilate the entire Jewish race. More than six million of God's chosen people were ruthlessly and inhumanely murdered. Could it be that the same Amalekite stronghold also influenced Hitler? Hitler was definitely deceived by demonic spirits and manifested pride and arrogance—just like Haman did. He demanded that people bow down and pay him homage in every situation—just like Haman. Hitler thrived on power, prestige and authority and destroyed everyone who exemplified insubordination—just like Haman tried to do.

Satan is in direct opposition to the plans and purposes of God, and so he uses the Amalekite stronghold to take over positions of authority. Satan searches our weak areas until he finds a gate of entrance. Because of Haman's pride, arrogance and desire for power and recognition, Satan had an open door to use him. When Satan can find someone like Haman, he moves in quickly to hinder and destroy God's anointed.

The Esthers of Today

Esther was determined for destiny. She was a woman who knew God, knew the destiny of God's people and was willing to sacrifice her life for it.

Each of us is a modern-day Esther. We have been prepared for such a time as this! We are coming forth in our due season to destroy the wickedness of the Amalekite. As Esther moved forward with godly focus, so must we. We must become even more determined for destiny so that we are empowered to thwart the plans of our enemies.

Modern-day Esthers are willing to sacrifice reputation, position and acceptance to approach the King and ask for His perfect will to be done. They will lay down their lives, if necessary, to pioneer a new truth. They are the ones who see into the future and destiny of the Church. They toss fear to the side and are willing to die for the cause of Christ.

There are many Esthers in today's churches and ministries, but they are being hindered greatly by the Amalekite strongholds. In order to achieve destiny for God's people, we must destroy the wickedness of the Amalekite by pressing into greater levels of intimacy with the Lord. Through our intimate times of fellowship and prayer, the Lord will speak strategies that will defeat the Amalekite spirit. Though the destiny thief seeks to destroy our promises, he will not steal the birthings of the Holy Spirit if we remain in intimacy.

Though we may be weary and have little strength to continue toward vision, God promises to bring the vision into reality. His Word states that He does not bring the seed (promise) to the time of birthing without bringing it fully forth:

> Shall I bring to the birth, and not cause to bring forth? saith the LORD: shall I cause to bring forth, and shut the womb? saith thy God. Rejoice ye with Jerusalem, and be glad with her, all ye that love her: rejoice for joy with her, all ye that mourn for her: That ye may suck, and be satisfied with the breasts of her consolations; that ye may milk out, and be delighted with the abundance of her glory.
>
> Isaiah 66:9–11

Saints, it is time to take a firm stand against the Amalekite stronghold so that our generations can experience their godly destiny. God was faithful to Esther, and He will be faithful to us. The seeds of destiny will be fulfilled, and He will rebuke the devourer for our sake. He is a God of His Word. What the Lord promises, He will fulfill.

Esthers, step forth, confident that God will do a saving work through you!

Nine

The Seduction of the Religious Spirit

When the Pharisees saw it, they said unto his disciples, Why eateth your Master with publicans and sinners?

Matthew 9:11

The sound of the phone ringing at two o'clock in the morning startled me from a deep sleep. My husband threw his arm toward the nightstand, attempting to locate the light switch. He knocked the receiver onto the floor in his hasty attempt to answer the phone.

My heart began to pound. A phone call in the middle of the night could only mean an emergency.

"He-l-l-o?" Barely awake, Mickey answered the call and then went silent as he listened. It was my father. He told Mickey that Mother was vomiting blood, and they were rushing her to the emergency room.

My heart sank. *What? Why is she vomiting blood?* We threw on clothes and met my parents at the hospital.

A series of tests proved that Mother had lung cancer. The doctors scheduled surgery to remove a third of both lungs. Though there was a malignant tumor in only one of the lungs, preventive measures were recommended to secure both lungs against future malignancy. Naturally, the entire family was devastated by the physician's report.

My sister, Pam, was the first to rise up in great faith. Her first words were in confidence that God would perform a miracle. The rest of the family, including my mother, concurred. Though all of us were shaken in our faith, at that point there was nowhere to look but up. We began to pray.

Another biopsy was scheduled in two days. The doctor released my mother to go home and rest. She would return to the hospital for the biopsy and then remain there for the surgery. It was during those two days that God began to speak to both of my parents and our entire family.

I remember being in my mother's den, sitting on her sofa. Pam began to declare the healing power of the Lord and that it was God's will to heal Mother from cancer. I listened intently, watching Mother's face as she contemplated Pam's words. She and my father both began to nod their heads in agreement. Mother needed a miracle, and we all knew it.

Pam laid hands upon Mother and prayed the prayer of faith. She had a measure of faith that even I needed. As she finished praying, I also began to pray. Together we bound the plans of the enemy and loosed God's healing touch upon her lungs. We cursed the cancerous tumor to the root and commanded that root to dislodge from her lungs. We proclaimed her healing and reminded my mother of God's promises of healing.

I later drove home praying in tongues. I was worried, shaken and still trying to stand on God's promises. Her biopsy would be the next day. *God will have to move,* I reassured myself.

On the way to the hospital the next morning I was hindered by traffic jams. At every turn I was delayed. I became more and more frustrated as I attempted to get to the hospital and be with my mother. I wanted to be with her during this crisis but instead found myself getting farther and farther behind. Unfortunately I arrived fifteen minutes late.

I hurried into the outpatient section and rushed to the second floor. Trying to find the proper room, I noticed Mother's doctor standing in the hallway. I moved toward him to ask if he was about to perform the procedure, thinking he was running behind as well. But as I approached I noticed he was staring intently into a glass jar.

"Doctor," I inquired, "have you already done the biopsy?"

No answer. He just continued to stare into the jar, which held some type of solution. I moved in closer to see what was in this jar. I noticed it looked strange and black. It had long tentacles or feelers of some type.

"I can't believe it," he said. "I simply can't believe it!"

"What?" I pushed for a clear answer.

The doctor was obviously stunned. He began to shake his head in total disbelief. "We just performed a biopsy of your mother's left lung. The tumor was even larger than I anticipated. It was 'angry,' which means it was definitely growing and malignant. When I began to scrape with the instrument used for a biopsy, your mother coughed abruptly. As she coughed, the tumor completely dislodged from her lung. I went in for a small biopsy, and now the entire tumor is here in this jar!"

Still in total amazement, he continued, "Not only that, but where the tentacles of the tumor were, the lung immediately healed over with fresh, pink skin. I looked again, and only fresh, pink, new tissue is there where the tumor was!"

Tears immediately filled my eyes and spilled over onto my face. *God did it*, I thought to myself. *God did it!*

I glanced into the room, and there was my mother still on the surgical table. Her hands were lifted into the air; she was praising God. She knew she had experienced a miracle. Over and over the words "Thank You, Jesus" filled the air.

Suddenly she jumped off the table and began to run up and down the hallway of the second floor. My once reserved, little mother, who always hesitated to share her faith, was approaching everyone on the floor with her testimony: "Jesus healed me! Jesus healed me!" she testified to everyone in her path.

The doctor smiled at her excitement. He did not attempt to hinder her excitement. In fact, none of the staff even considered pointing her toward the exit doors. Clearly, all had witnessed a miracle.

"Here, you might want to keep this," the doctor said as he handed me a picture of the tumor in the jar. I looked for several minutes at the picture. Black with very long feelers and roots, the tumor was demonic-looking. Obviously this tumor had attempted to permanently lodge itself and spread its deadly infection. As I focused on this miracle, the memory of Pam cursing the tumor to the "root" ran through my mind. God had most definitely answered our request. He had removed that angry, demonic tumor from the root—and now the enemy's plan was fully contained in a jar with a closed lid!

I still have the picture of that tumor. Periodically I retrieve it from the bureau and am reminded of God's miracle-working power!

Miracles Are for Today

Miracles did not cease when the apostles died. A religious spirit will try to convince believers that it did.

For years I attended a certain denominational church that preaches dispensationalism—the teaching that miracles died with the apostles—and I believed that error. When I began to understand the full Gospel, I realized that God is the same, yesterday, today and forever! If He healed yesterday, He will heal today. My mother was proof of that. And I have further proof. My sister has been healed of ovarian tumors several times. My mother died once of a heart attack while in an ambulance, and God brought her back to life. He has miraculously resurrected my mother from the jaws of death at least five times. We have witnessed His faithfulness over and over.

God wants to do even more miracles through each of us. Just as He flowed through the apostles in instances documented throughout the Scriptures, He desires to flow through today's believers. But there is a stronghold of doubt and unbelief that hinders the greater levels of faith that are needed.

The Religious Spirit

In chapter 5 we discussed how God is requiring obedience from today's leaders, and how we can no longer fear man or remain in religious tradition. In order to embrace more of His Spirit, God requires us to let go of old behavior, thought patterns and traditions. The religious spirit, however, will do all it can to contest and hinder major breakthroughs in the Spirit.

Remember how the religious spirit operated against Jesus? The spirit, operating in the Pharisees, instructed Jesus that He could not heal on the Sabbath and that He could not eat with the sinners (see Matthew 9:11; 12:10; Mark 2:16; 3:2; Luke 5:30; 6:7; 13:14; 14:1–5; John 5:16–18; 7:22–23; 9:14–16). The Pharisees were pious and prideful in their traditions but did not know God.

The religious spirit was active during Jesus' ministry and continues to operate today in our modern churches. Religious spirits are secure in "old order" and protest any new revelation from God—while God is saying, "Wait a minute. I would like to say something!" Religious spirits promote pride, arrogance and religious mind-sets and work through people in local churches. The voice of a religious spirit speaking through people sounds like:

"I don't believe healing is for today."

"God doesn't perform miracles."

"We must pray for God's will, not a miracle."

"Speaking in tongues is of the devil."

"I don't believe in that holy-roller stuff."

"What do you mean you lay hands on the sick?"

"You mean your church services are more than 45 minutes long?"

"Women should be silent in the church."

"We should not sing in the Spirit."

"I don't believe in deliverance. Even though Jesus died on the cross to deliver me, I still feel crazy at times!"

"Surely you don't dance in church, do you?"

"You actually clap in church?"

Or in a Spirit-filled congregation, the religious spirit may sound like:

"I can hear from God better than the senior leader."

"I am a prophet of God; listen to me."

"I alone hear God better than all. Hear me only."

"There are no prophets or apostles today."

"I don't believe in spiritual warfare."

"The only anointed and true Word is the King James translation."

Many congregations today, for example, are teaching cutting-edge, breakthrough revelations concerning the power of deliverance. But there are multitudes who totally disagree with the need for deliverance. This group believes that the blood of Jesus healed everything when they became born again. They profess that their attitudes and behavior do not necessitate deliverance, yet they are bound up in shame, guilt, mental torment, addictions and various forms of sickness. Those who protest deliverance need it the most, for a demon actually has convinced them that they do not need deliverance.

The truth is that Jesus did die for our sins, but that is only one phase of our blessing. There is more for us to experience—such as complete deliverance and complete salvation—which involves walking into greater levels of healing and wholeness. Measures of physical breakthroughs and layers of deliverance can occur at different levels of spiritual maturity. So as we grow in Christ, we are healed more completely and become more fully whole. Being born again in and of itself assures our salvation, but it does not free us completely of the enemy's influence; we must walk that out as we grow in the Lord. Deliverance, then, is greatly needed in the Church.

Another example of a religious mind-set, as I mentioned briefly above, is the belief that the only anointed and true Word is the King James translation. Several years ago a gentleman approached me because I used a translation of the Bible other than the King James. Most of the time, I teach from the King James, but that day I used another translation for greater clarity. Immediately after the service this man told me that God only approved the King James and that I was teaching deception. This is the voice of a religious stronghold at work attempting to bind up the Body of Christ with legalism.

Religion says that we have to speak a certain way, pray a certain way, believe a certain way, confess a certain way, proclaim a certain way and even prophesy a certain way. To find God we have to get past that mind-set. We must defeat the religious stronghold that binds us in legalism and death, and instead we must seek the Spirit of God, which releases life and empowerment.

Religious Spirit→Seducing Spirit→Sin→ Doubt

A religious spirit always tries to convince us to compromise. It is closely associated with seducing spirits and unclean spirits. Once the religious spirit convinces us to compromise, the seducing spirit is then able to lure us into areas of sin and uncleanness, which lead quickly to doubt and unbelief. These spirits bring defilement and apostasy. They work against our minds and feed thoughts such as:

"Go ahead and sin. No one will ever know."

"Life was easier before you were a Christian."

"Go back into the world!"

"Go ahead, take a drink. God won't care."

"Cheating on your wife is not the unpardonable sin!"

The Religious Spirit Prevents New Wine

Always when God is bringing forth a new truth, the religious spirit rises up and manifests. We see this in our personal lives when we are struggling with walking in faith. Just at the time of a major spiritual breakthrough in a person's life, the familiar voice of this seducing, unclean spirit sounds like:

"God doesn't really care about you. Give up."

"You are unworthy to receive any breakthrough. Throw in the towel now."

"You will never receive a promise from God. Just look at you. You are unworthy and worthless."

"Why don't you just speak it out loud? God is a liar, and you have been deceived with all this 'faith' stuff!"

"This mountain is too big for your God."

We also see the religious spirit rise up when the corporate Body is facing a major breakthrough, and it begins to dictate how God moves. If we allow God's Spirit to minister as He desires, the religious spirit immediately challenges us to go back to what is comfortable and we "box in" God. This is because He is moving differently than before, challenging our mind-sets and comfort zones. Many pastors are so afraid of losing control that they do not allow any tongues, prophecy or laying on of hands for healing and miracles. This is very sad because the Holy Spirit desires to speak and move freely, ministering life to us.

Religious tradition is legalism, and the Word says that the law brings death. Religious tradition and mind-sets dictate loss of faith and spiritual revelation, resulting in spiritual death. Only the Spirit of God releases life and empowerment—whether in a person's personal life or in a church service.

God is seeking to release the new wine of the Holy Spirit. When Jesus spoke on the new wine (see Matthew 9:17; Mark 2:22; Luke 5:37–39), He was attempting to break the disciples free of tradition and mind-sets. He actually came to challenge them concerning their belief system and religious structures. Jesus was determined to provoke spirits of religion and tradition by working miracles and speaking truth! He knew that His present truth messages would cause a ripping and a tearing of their religious systems.

New Wine Requires New Wineskins

A majority of God's children think they want the new wine—until they are challenged to change their thinking! When new truths are taught, people begin to feel uncomfortable. They do not want to allow God to challenge them to change. Instead, they bail out and go back to the old things.

Jesus said that once someone has drunk the old wine, they do not want new wine. This is very true. Old habits die hard. Old belief systems die hard. We continually box God into a formula. We do not fully understand that though He does not change, He loves change! He is continually changing us into His image.

As the Scriptures tell us, this new wine requires new wineskins. And there will be a ripping and a tearing until we choose to change: "No one puts new wine into old wineskins; otherwise the new wine will burst the skins and it will be spilled out, and the skins will be ruined" (Luke 5:37, NASB). God desires to move differently than before, and this "new move" challenges every mind-set. God wants control. When His Spirit moves in, it rips up and tears down the old religious order. I have observed many areas of ripping and tearing within God's Church.

When I first saw it in our own congregation, I began to pray for new wineskins—for God's people to receive fresh revelation. I fasted and prayed to avoid the ripping and tearing. But the Lord told me that in order for me to see that our church was not ready for the new move of the Spirit, He allowed and actually caused areas to rip and tear!

I did not want the ripping and tearing! No pastor wants his or her congregation to be ripped and torn apart. But I realized that God was pointing out a truth that we as a congregation were not embracing. I learned that if God was pouring out new wine and there was a tearing, then something needed fixing.

In order to battle the religious spirit, we must prepare ourselves to be new wineskins. We must be ready to hold the new movement of the Holy Spirit that God desires to give us—both personally and corporately.

Embrace the New Wine

God is causing a ripping and tearing in the Church wineskins. He is giving us a needed wake-up call. He wants to bring change. To change us, He may change the order of our church services so that He can move in a greater dimension of His power!

If a ripping and tearing is happening in your church, do not blame the devil. Press into God and ask Him how you can accommodate the Holy Spirit more. And then, after you ask the Holy Spirit to come into your meetings, let Him move. If you are asking Him to come but you are not ready for His fullness, your congregation might rip and tear.

If you are not experiencing this ripping and tearing in your life, church or ministry, do not despair! The enemy loves to place shame on God's chosen. Simply back off, seek God and ask Him to begin to speak clearly into those areas He desires to change. All of us have control issues. Remember that the Holy Spirit wants full control.

In every new area of Holy Spirit-directed change, you will be challenged with mind-sets and religious tradition. Religious spirits will rise up against you. Jezebel spirits of control will attempt to control and manipulate your decisions. The accuser of the brethren will falsely testify against you. If these spirits begin to operate, then you are probably on the right track.

Don't quit now! Become determined for destiny! You're moving in the right direction and embracing new wine. I pray for the grace of God for each of us as He leads us into all truth.

Witchcraft and the Religious Spirit

Religious spirits often manifest through witchcraft. By now you should be realizing that witchcraft is a manifestation of all seducing spirits. The religious spirit is no different.

Witchcraft is a work of the flesh and is forbidden in the Scriptures. We are instructed never to partake of any form of witchcraft. We discussed this briefly in chapter 5, but when considering the religious spirit it is important to look again at the fact that God says rebellion is a form of witchcraft.

> For rebellion is as the sin of witchcraft, and stubbornness is as iniquity and idolatry. Because thou hast rejected the word of the LORD, he hath also rejected thee from being king.
>
> 1 Samuel 15:23

How often have we been as King Saul and kicked against God's plans? When we resist His directions and instructions, we are in rebellion—witchcraft! The religious spirit, then, lures us into resisting God's plan, and thus we usher in witchcraft.

One area where a religious spirit turns easily into witchcraft is intercession. Intercessors with a religious spirit are deceived. Directed by this spirit, they will pray soulish prayers targeted against leaders in their church. They will feel that they have the proper direction for the church and will attempt to force their "direction received through prayer" upon the leadership. If the leadership is not ready to move out on the unction of the intercessor, he/she will at times feel rejected and angry. Rather than submit, the intercessor will pray for his or her own will out of rebellion and lack of submission to delegated authority.

In the beginning the intercessors' motives may have been innocent, but in the process their prayers take on a form of charismatic witchcraft. Charismatic witchcraft is prayer based upon an individual's isolated and personal insight, desire and will. This form of witchcraft hinders godly authority and a move of the Holy Spirit.

If you are an intercessor, please remember to remain accountable and teachable. Do not allow a religious, judgmental stronghold to overtake you whenever God is releasing change and transformation. (For more information on charismatic witchcraft, I recommend Gary Greenwald's book, _Seductions Exposed._)

But there are also genuine witches and sorcerers who pray against churches and ministers. They practice incantations and satanic rituals that attempt to hinder the plans and purposes of God. Satan has principalities and powers at work against God's Church. Many different spiritual assignments are released through demons attempting to abort the plans and purposes of God's chosen.

We must resist rebelling against God's leaders and those He has assigned over us, and we must resist rebelling against God's plans for us. To rebel against those God has placed in authority or His will for our lives opens the doors to many demonic assignments.

Evil Reports against Others

Rebellion is not the only sin that gives religious spirits an opening. Religious spirits also team up with the accuser of the brethren to speak evil reports concerning others—especially against leadership.

Wherever there is negativity when God begins to pour out His new wine, wineskins begin to rip and tear. His truth will not compete with old mind-sets and tradition. Negativity stops a fresh move of the Spirit because negativity gives place to doubt and unbelief. Doubt and unbelief abort breakthroughs planned by the Spirit.

Once evil reports are released, defilement follows. Remember: We are not to touch the unclean thing. If we open the door to defilement, we open doors to unclean spirits.

 An evil report involves false accusation, a distortion of facts and bogus information. Most of the time these falsehoods are communicated with wrong motives intended to cause harm to someone or his or her reputation. At first the falsehood may be received in total innocence, but if it is repeated it later brings contamination. An evil report is similar to an evil germ that becomes active upon infection. If not treated, the infection moves into a disease and possible death. The same happens to us when we partake of evil reports. Whether we receive the report or give the report, the defilement is the same.

 Evil reports take the form of gossip, whispering, slander, backbiting, tale-bearing and being a busybody. Reports often develop from deep wounds, jealousy, bitterness, rebellion, envy and pride. Those who have been wounded by authority are often bitter and begin to speak negatively about leaders with hurtful intent. When jealousy finds its place in the Body of Christ, some become fault-finders.

Once defilement occurs, symptoms of disease begin to develop. Symptoms of the infection are

1. believing the evil reports to be true without going to the correct sources for truth;
2. forming negative opinions and spreading rumors;
3. judging others based on a negative report;
4. focusing on the negative in other areas.

Left untreated, these symptoms can result in disease—both spiritually and physically.

Did you realize that bitterness causes physical illness? I knew a man who was extremely full of bitterness. He refused to move forward beyond a victim mentality. He was struck with severe arthritis. The Lord gave me a word of knowledge concerning his bitterness and unforgiveness. After he received truth, the Lord delivered him from the demonic oppression caused by the bitterness and unforgiveness, and he was healed.

The Bible warns us to be consistent to forgive those who have hurt us. Forgiveness releases the love of God and the fruits of healing to our hearts and bodies. Forgiveness erases bitterness.

If in your heart you feel the urge to spread negative reports and you find yourself bitter, then it is time to repent. Ask for forgiveness for listening to lies and negativity. Ask the Lord to forgive you for allowing that evil spirit to work through you. You will know that your heart is cleansed whenever you begin to grieve over negative reports. You will become saddened to hear negative words spoken about leaders or those you respect and admire. By quickly examining our own lives for failures, we will derail Satan's plans to use us in this fashion again.

We will never reach destiny if we choose to believe negative reports. The only way to move forth into our destiny is to believe God and His Word. This involves believing what He says about others and us. Rather than remaining critical of others, begin confessing what God has declared over their lives. Believe me: It will make a difference in your heart! Soon you will notice your attitude—and motive—toward them changing.

Life penetrates our bodies and minds when we choose to believe the Word of God. Defilement and death are the results of negative reports. Be on guard, dear one. The enemy goes forth as a roaring lion to devour you. Choose to believe the Lord and experience your victory!

Repent Now

Has the religious spirit had a stronghold over your life? If so, how? Write it below.

Now write a strategy of how you plan to overcome and fulfill your destiny.

Repent from having mind-sets concerning the move of the Holy Spirit. Receive empowerment from the Holy Spirit to claim and possess your mountain of promise. Write out your repentance below.

Are you struggling with loving others? If so, write below what God has said concerning them. After writing down the positive reports from the Lord, pray over each Scripture, asking God to heal your heart toward those people.

Break Loose of the Religious Spirit

It is time for us to break loose of the religious spirit that has controlled so much of our lives. We must not allow the religious spirit to keep us from experiencing everything—

every miracle—that God intends to give us. Let us not be Pharisees, who sought to stop the Son of God from acting. Let us not be bound in legalism and death. We must not allow any area of defilement or uncleanness to dictate our lives. We must not allow the stronghold of doubt and unbelief to hinder us from walking in the greater levels of faith that are needed to usher in the full power of God's Holy Spirit. Let us seek the Spirit of God, who releases life and empowerment. Let us prepare ourselves to be new wineskins who are ready to hold the new movement of the Holy Spirit that God desires to give us.

We have a higher calling, a destiny to fulfill in God. Let us have the spirit of Joshua and Caleb. Let us be determined for destiny and embrace the new wine!

Ten

The Seduction of the Unclean Spirit

> And there was in their synagogue a man with an unclean spirit; and he cried out, saying, Let us alone; what have we to do with thee, thou Jesus of Nazareth? art thou come to destroy us? I know thee who thou art, the Holy One of God.
>
> Mark 1:23–24

When we think of someone being *unclean* we often describe him or her as "dirty," "nasty" and even "untouchable" due to the filth to which they have been exposed. Webster's Dictionary defines *unclean* as "being morally or spiritually impure; infected with a harmful supernatural contagion."[1]

The instructions from God have always been to touch not the unclean thing (see 2 Corinthians 6:17). We are instructed to remove ourselves from every unclean influence and become holy and blameless before the Lord.

The unclean spirit is a tremendous stronghold in the Body of Christ. Sin causes defilement, and defilement closes the doors to spiritual breakthroughs. For this reason unclean spirits cry out, "Leave us alone!" They do not want us to deal with them, for they desire to continue doing what they are doing—defiling God's people and influencing them to continue in sin and spiritual adultery.

The spirits want to persuade us to believe that there is no power in the name of Jesus, and especially that there is no need for deliverance. Unclean spirits know the name of Jesus and the power it contains, and that is why their goal is to deceive many into believing that they do not need deliverance.

Deliverance from unclean spirits is absolutely necessary in the Body of Christ. Only when we are cleansed from unclean spirits can we be used to our fullest potential in the Body of Christ and pursue with complete abandon the destiny He intends for each of us.

Characteristics of the Unclean Spirit

Many people have asked me how I know when an unclean spirit is operating. The main way to determine if a spirit is at work is through spiritual discernment. With proper discernment any spirit is recognized. But certain characteristics are common when an unclean spirit is manifesting within a church congregation or individual, and those characteristics are easy to identify.

1. Exhibits an Unkempt Appearance and Defiled Speech

The most obvious characteristic to the natural eye is a lack of personal hygiene. Individuals will appear unkempt in their appearance and dirty or filthy. Often, cursing or telling dirty jokes defiles their speech. These are vivid representations of the unclean spirit at work.

This characteristic is easily seen in a person's home. I have visited homes that were so unkempt that I wanted to leave the premises as quickly as possible. In most cases like this, an unclean spirit has become a stronghold in the home.

A continual pattern of natural uncleanness almost always means there is a spiritual root.

2. Evidenced by Lust, Sexual Perversion and Pornography

An unclean spirit exists wherever there is lust and perversion. Many times pornography is a stronghold, as well as sexual deviation. Incest, adultery, masturbation and twisted, perverted imaginations are evidences of an unclean spirit working in someone's life.

3. Manifests in Rigid Belief Systems

Jesus addressed the Pharisees as being unclean due to their belief system. He said that one is defiled not by what is eaten, but because of what is on the inside (see Mark 7:15). The Pharisees believed and trusted in their religious order. They trusted in their fasting, prayers and religious structure. Within congregations today an unclean spirit manifests in the same ways as it did in the Pharisees—in rigid belief systems that are not open to the new word and move of God and that hinder spiritual breakthrough.

4. Encourages Doubt and Unbelief

The Jewish believers were saturated with doubt and unbelief, and Jesus continually rebuked them for their lack of faith. Jesus called these "religious" men a den of vipers and unclean. In Matthew 12:33–34, Jesus told the religious leaders that they were evil and had been corrupted. He specifically addressed them as having corrupt and rotten (defiled) fruit.

If the fruit is corrupt and defiled, then the entire tree is corrupt. In other words, there was an evil spirit, a strong territorial spirit, over the religious system during Jesus' time. And that unclean spirit is still active today in our church congregations. Wherever there is doubt and unbelief, an unclean spirit is at work.

5. Influences as a Regional (Territorial) Stronghold

An unclean spirit is a regional stronghold. The spirit has been allowed to influence heavily a large region or territory due to spiritual doors that have been opened to it in that area.

It is very important that we recognize the influence of the unclean spirit as it gains demonic governmental control over large areas at a time. Jesus Himself opposed the unclean spirit in the region of Decapolis, which was a territory composed of several cities. The unclean spirit had manifested in that specific region as a territorial stronghold. When an unclean spirit moves into its assigned district, it takes over entire families, neighborhoods, cities and even states and countries. When it targets a local church, many in the congregation might manifest unclean thoughts, areas of sexual defilement, perversion, sexual addictions, sickness and disease. It also manifests in congregational doubt and unbelief that hinder church breakthrough.

Several years ago I had a dream concerning an unclean spirit. At the time of the dream our church congregation was experiencing much turmoil. I discerned that an unclean spirit was attacking the young adults. I quickly went into prayer to discern how to dismantle the false authority of the defiling spirit. The Lord answered me with a dream about a strongman who had a spirit similar to Saul in the Old Testament. The strongman lived in a very dark castle and rode a black horse. The strongman was dressed in full armor. In the dream the "Saul" spirit spoke to me and said that he had a plan to destroy all Israel. Then I awoke.

Since I travel and teach on dreams and visions and their interpretations, this particular dream was very easy for me to interpret. The dark castle represented a stronghold of darkness. The spirit of Saul represented the old religious order, the old way. Horses most often represent strength. In this case, it was a dark horse, which represented the strength of darkness. Saul had on full armor, and this represented warfare. He proclaimed that this attack was not simply against our small congregation but against all Israel. In other words, it was a regional attack.

My husband and I are an apostolic-prophetic team who apostolically oversee several churches and regions for Christian International Ministries. At the time of the dream we were one week away from hosting a large prophetic conference in Dallas, Texas. We began to alert the entire region concerning the dream. We warned them against any possible manifestations of the unclean spirit. The entire network in Texas began to fast and pray. At the time of the conference we experienced a powerful manifestation of God's presence. We corporately bound the unclean spirit over our state and loosed God's prophetic-apostolic mantle. It was one of the most powerful conferences we ever hosted! The plans against our congregation ceased quickly after the conference was over, and we proceeded toward destiny in His purposes. Hallelujah!

6. Keeps People in Dead Places, Bondage and Mental Torment

Stagnant waters breed mosquitoes, and these insects suck life-giving blood from their victims. In the same way, the unclean spirit sucks the life from believers by containing them in old patterns and dead places or areas that are defiled.

When the Body of Christ chooses to remain stagnant, they are open prey to the enemy. These gruesome "insects" steal the life from them. In order to avoid these bloodsuckers, we must keep moving. Move forward! When we stop moving as God directs, we are in danger of defilement. We then move easily into rebellion, and rebellion opens doors to witchcraft and many other demonic spirits.

Observe what the Scriptures say about the unclean spirit in Mark 5:

> And when he was come out of the ship, immediately there met him out of the tombs a man with an *unclean spirit*, who had his dwelling among the tombs; and no man could bind him, no, not with chains: because that he had been often *bound* with fetters and chains, and the chains had been plucked asunder by him, and the fetters broken in pieces: neither could any man tame him.
>
> Mark 5:2–4 (emphasis mine)

Notice that this man with the unclean spirit lived in the tombs, a place of death and decay. He had been bound often. The demoniac was mentally tormented, and no man could reason with him. He was completely controlled by an unclean spirit. The Scripture goes on to say that he would cry night and day and literally cut himself with stones.

 I have counseled women who have been so tormented by the unclean spirit that they have cut themselves with knives and other sharp instruments, just as the man with the unclean spirit. When this spirit invades a congregation, the cutting is a bit different—Christians actually go after each other! They use cutting words against the leadership. They falsely accuse each other and say words that cut deep into the hearts of others.

Unclean spirits desire to keep us bound spiritually. They want to keep us in the "tombs," surrounded by death and decay. They want to keep us in torment and completely control us so that we "cut" ourselves and others.

7. Promotes Words of Death and Evil Reports

"Death and life are in the power of the tongue: and they that love it shall eat the fruit thereof" (Proverbs 18:21). Many words of death, therefore, are released when an unclean spirit is active. Words easily become curses and death assignments when fueled by jealousy, hatred and rage—all manifestations of an unclean spirit.

Unclean spirits cause us to focus on the faults of others rather than searching for areas of our own personal defilement. When we become negative, lash out verbally and disconnect, most likely an unclean spirit is active. Remember: Jesus stated that it was not the uncleanness on the outside but on the inside that defiled the man. Believers need to search their hearts continually for areas of defilement, and be cautious what they speak and release to others.

8. Aborts and Separates Destiny

The unclean spirit separated the demoniac and placed him in a graveyard, where no one wanted to live. The man lived alone and became lonely and crazy.

Unclean spirits separate us from our destiny. They convince Christians that they do not belong. They devise plans to cause offenses in order to separate believers from spiritual authority and like believers.

The Scriptures say that where there is unity there is life. Dead places, therefore, promote disunity and separation. Whenever an unclean spirit attacks a church congregation, the first thing I notice is the disunity among the people. The next thing is the dismantling of authority within the congregation. Slanderous words are hurled against the leaders, and then the spiritual covering breaks down and people begin to disconnect. Suddenly there is a breach among the brethren, and the lack of trust in leadership causes an exodus or church split. If believers do not lock back into God's plan, their destiny is aborted.

9. Travels with Other Spirits

Unclean spirits often travel with a multitude of other spirits. The demon-possessed man in the tombs, for example, was controlled by a demon that identified himself as *Legion*, indicating that many demons were at work.

I have discerned that unclean spirits often travel with the Jezebel and Absalom spirits and religious spirits. Absalom spirits promote disunity and slander against true godly authority. Jezebel promotes idolatry, false belief systems, fornication and sexual perversion. All these stain the Body of Christ with sin and defilement.

10. Sickness, Disease and Death Become Generational Patterns

When an unclean spirit attacks a church or family, sickness, disease and death often become continual problems. We call this a generational stronghold of an unclean spirit. In such cases we most often find long-standing disease and repeated acts of sexual perversion. Even children are influenced, and a generational pattern of an unclean spirit in them manifests as masturbation, pornography and foul language. When an unclean spirit attacks a generation, the stronghold remains intact until it is bound up and then broken off through prayer and deliverance.

11. Robs Faith and Determination by Wearing You Out

An unclean spirit will rob your determination for destiny by separating and isolating you and then beginning to wear you out. In the past, when I was under an evil assignment from an unclean spirit, I would become absolutely exhausted. As a result of being physically drained I would become ill. This is the enemy's plan: to cause burnout, fatigue and illness.

The enemy's job is to wear out the saints. He targets you with whatever stronghold will gain victory, isolate you from the Body and then move in for the kill. This is why it is very important to remain connected to the Body when under attack. If you become separated, then you are an easy prey for the enemy.

12. Separates from Destiny Links and Causes Loss of Vision

If the unclean stronghold succeeds in separating you from the rest of the Body or separating you from your destiny links, then it will cause you to lose vision. Vision only comes when we are connected. When we become disconnected, it is too easy to lose focus and vision, and then we will perish. Life and vitality are the fruits of pursuing vision. When there is no vision, there is no energy to go forth and accomplish destiny.

> And the LORD answered me, and said, Write the vision, and make it plain upon tables, that *he may run* that readeth it. For the vision is yet for an appointed time, but at the end it shall speak, and not lie: though it tarry, wait for it; because it will surely come, it will not tarry.
>
> Habakkuk 2:2–3 (emphasis mine)

Driving Out the Unclean Spirit

Since doubt and unbelief always manifest when an unclean spirit is in the midst, the way to uproot its power and entanglement is to begin to speak God's Word in faith. When this spirit is at work, fear attempts to enter into the hearts of people. Take a firm stand, therefore, and remain in faith.

Luke 9:37–42 documents the disciples' attempt to drive an unclean spirit from a child. As they tried to cast it out, they could not. Instead the spirit tore at the child and caused foaming at the mouth. Jesus boldly addressed their lack of faith and called the disciples perverse: "And Jesus answering said, O faithless and perverse generation, how long shall I be with you, and suffer you? Bring thy son hither" (verse 41).

When they attempted to cast out the unclean spirit, the disciples dealt with doubt and unbelief. This confirms that doubt and unbelief manifest when this stronghold attacks.

Jesus addressed them as faithless and perverse. The word *perverse* in this passage translates as "distorted" and "to turn aside" (from the right path through corruption) and "oppose or plot against the saving purposes and plans of God."[2] This translation clearly shows how the unclean spirit causes its victim to turn away from destiny and oppose the purposes and plans that God has for him or her.

Also required to destroy the unclean spirit are clean hands and pure hearts. Clean hands represent freedom from guilt—innocence, blamelessness and being cut off from sin. Pure hearts are those that seek righteousness and seek to follow the Lord completely:

Who shall ascend into the hill of the LORD? or who shall stand in his holy place? He that hath clean hands, and a pure heart; who hath not lifted up his soul unto vanity, nor sworn deceitfully. He shall receive the blessing from the LORD, and righteousness from the God of his salvation. This is the generation of them that seek him, that seek thy face, O Jacob. Selah.

Psalm 24:3–6

As pastors, we at times have called our entire congregation to fasting and prayer. We have cleansed our land by praying over the church property. We have repented from generational curses or any areas of defilement the Lord reveals. One season we fasted and prayed and then called the intercessors together as we poured oil upon our property. We sprinkled salt upon the earth, symbolizing purity and cleansing of our land.

As we repent, we cleanse ourselves from iniquities and curses from past generations. We pray that the Lord would cleanse and purify our hearts so that we might experience a higher level of His glory. The only way for us to ascend to a higher level and experience His greater presence is through the cleansing of our hearts and hands.

Freedom from an Unclean Spirit Depends upon These Actions:

R ecognize it for what it is: Defilement!

R epent for all areas of the defilement.

R emember His Word and ways to ensure proper cleansing and healing.

R ighteousness is the right choice.

R eel in your thoughts.

R enew your mind.

R egard righteous living as a necessity.

And Utterly Destroy All!

Do Not Look Back

When God delivered Lot and his family from Sodom and Gomorrah, they were not to look back on the cities. When Lot's wife just could not let go of the "old thing" and looked back, she was destroyed.

God is calling you out! When He calls you away from an old lifestyle, a city or a relationship, you cannot look back over your shoulder. Let go and separate yourself unto Him, and He will be faithful to save you.

Are there areas of defilement in your life—areas that might give the unclean spirits an open door? Take time right now to repent of your sin. Repentance will cleanse you from all unrighteousness. Sanctify yourself by the washing of His powerful Word. And then, dear saints, do not look back!

11
Eleven

The Jezebel Spirit

Notwithstanding I have a few things against thee, because thou sufferest that woman Jezebel, which calleth herself a prophetess, to teach and to seduce my servants to commit fornication, and to eat things sacrificed unto idols.

Revelation 2:20

I felt a chill run down my spine as she approached the altar.

Oh, no! I told the Lord. *Surely she does not have another prophetic word!*

She moved in for the kill, searching for a microphone. She stared straight at me, as if to intimidate me with her determination and imagined anointing. She bowed up her back, almost like an attacking cat, and stretching out her hand to get the microphone she said, "I have a word from God!"

I held my position as senior leader and pastor of our flock and began asking the Lord if I should allow her to prophesy. The intimidation from the Jezebel spirit arose to undermine my authority.

I knew the season had come when Mickey and I had to say no to her. We had tried on numerous occasions to give her loving correction, but she never received our counsel. Each time we had attempted to intervene, she retaliated. Based on past history with this woman, I knew that if I maintained my godly position and refused to allow her to "prophesy," she would cause strife and division within minutes of her rejection.

I fought through my fears of what I would be facing—long counseling sessions with her friends in the church, betrayal, lies and witchcraft—and said, "No, not this time."

Her cold eyes stared through me. She was not smiling and was definitely unhappy. This was truly the straw that broke the camel's back. My refusal to allow her to go to the microphone did not hinder her determination to speak her mind. Words that were obviously not of God began to flow out of her mouth. Then she prayed aloud in the spirit—but it was not the Spirit of God speaking. The false tongue bore no witness, and there was no godly interpretation.

Though she would have enjoyed more attention by giving false direction through illegitimate authority, Mickey grabbed the microphone and took godly authority. She removed herself, went to her seat and snatched her children and husband from their seats. They all exited out the front doors.

The atmosphere was disturbed—actually defiled. A false prophetess had been in the house of God attempting to usurp and gain illegal authority. It had been a seven-month battle with a strong Jezebel spirit. I hoped it was over.

After the service, I was extremely grieved. I prayed, repented and mourned over this relationship. *Why couldn't I help her? We tried every way possible to bring healing and restoration.* I cried out for answers.

A few days later we experienced another fallout. Several couples had decided to leave with her. The Jezebel gathered her flock, which she had controlled, and they left for their new church. This had been the pattern for this particular group—moving from church to church, with Jezebel seeking a position of authority. The group entered into the next place wounded and unhealed, and ultimately left the next church the same way they entered—wounded and un-healed. This is because Jezebel will not receive correction and discipline. If this spirit cannot control a pastor and congregation, then it will not remain. A Jezebel seeks only those who can be controlled and manipulated.

Though it was sad to lose families, we could do nothing but release them. We had a clear word from the Lord that we were to tolerate no longer Jezebel's intimidation and control. God reminded us of His strict words to the church in Thyatira, which He rebuked for tolerating Jezebel:

And unto the angel of the church in Thyatira write; These things saith the Son of God, who hath his eyes like unto a flame of fire, and his feet are like fine brass; I know thy works, and charity, and service, and faith, and thy patience, and thy works; and the last to be more than the first. *Notwithstanding I have a few things against thee, because thou sufferest that woman Jezebel*, which calleth herself a prophetess, to teach and to *seduce* my servants to commit fornication, and to eat things sacrificed unto idols. And I gave her space to repent of her fornication; and *she repented not*. Behold, I will cast her into a bed, and them that commit adultery with her into great tribulation, except they repent of their deeds. And I will kill her children with death; and all the churches shall know that I am he which searcheth the reins and hearts: and I will give unto every one of you according to your works. But unto you I say, and unto the rest in Thyatira, as many as have not this doctrine, and which have not known the depths of Satan, as they speak; I will put upon you none other burden.

Revelation 2:18–24 (emphasis mine)

187

Jezebel and Her Seductions

We must search the Scriptures to understand the Jezebel spirit. Jezebel is mentioned in both the Old and New Testaments. In the Old Testament she was known as Jezebel, the queen, who attacked and murdered the prophets of God (see 1 Kings 18:4). Her name is mentioned again in the New Testament in Revelation 2:20. It is obvious that the Revelation passage is not speaking of the same physical woman from the Old Testament. Rather, the Scriptures are speaking of the spirit of Jezebel, which was operating within the Church. This same spirit operates through others today, infecting churches with its manipulation and control.

 In the Old Testament Jezebel murdered the prophets and intimidated Elijah to the point that he wanted to die. First Kings 18 documents that Elijah called down fire from heaven, slew the false prophets of Baal, prophesied and released rain after years of drought, and then outran Ahab's chariot into the entrance of Jezreel. Then in the very next chapter Jezebel was incensed and threatened to murder Elijah for all he had done. Instead of destroying Jezebel, as he had the false prophets, he took off running for his life. Talk about a spirit of intimidation in operation! You would think that after Elijah had just been empowered by God to destroy the altars of Baal and then chop off the heads of hundreds of false prophets, he would remain confident in his abilities. The threat and intimidating words of just one woman, however, sent him off on a 24-hour trip—nonstop—into the wilderness to hide in a cave (see 1 Kings 19:1–4). God had to call Elijah out from that dark place, speak life and direction to him, and empower him to move forward. The threat of Jezebel was so intimidating that if God had not called him out, Elijah may have spent the rest of his days in hiding.

I have had the same battle with Jezebel myself! The seducing spirit of Jezebel promotes what Bishop Hamon refers to as the "Persecution Complex." In his book *Prophets, Pitfalls and Principles*,[1] Bishop Bill Hamon exposes the intimidation and persecution that Elijah experienced. It was so strong that Elijah developed a persecution complex—the deception of being so overwhelmingly persecuted that one can run away from his destiny. Elijah had a destiny to hold steadfast and remain in his spiritual authority in the region. But when Jezebel came after him, he left his post, took the risk of aborting his destiny and ran in the opposite direction.

Have you been like me and like Elijah? Have you had an incredible breakthrough, only to find Jezebel knocking at your door? You answer the door and are greeted by intimidation, false accusations, fear, manipulation, control and seduction. The seducing spirit of Jezebel pulls us out of our divine destiny. It isolates us from our destiny links and our destiny.

A key insight into Jezebel's tactics is understanding how Elijah received her threatening words. By examining closely verse 3, we see that he actually envisioned his death:

> Then Jezebel sent a messenger unto Elijah, saying, So let the gods do to me, and more also, if I make not thy life as the life of one of them by to morrow about this time. And when he *saw* that, he arose, and went for his life.
>
> 1 Kings 19:2–3 (emphasis mine)

Notice the emphasis here: Elijah *saw* his destruction! He connected a "picture" to her intimidating words, and seeing the destruction sent him running.

Jezebel's words are intended to seduce and ultimately to steal destiny. Her intimidating threats take a firm grip not only upon our emotions but also upon our minds. The mental torment is so strong that we envision defeat, hopelessness and despair before it even happens. When we hear her threatening words we are tempted to follow the same pattern as Elijah:

1. experience an overwhelming fear of dread and despair;
2. run from destiny;
3. find ourselves in the wilderness wishing to die;
4. become exhausted from the mental torment and running away from destiny; and
5. find ourselves in another 40-day/40-night experience where God is calling us out of the cave (see verses 4–9).

In the Old Testament the Jezebel spirit is portrayed as:

- a murderer
- a thief
- an intimidator
- a manipulator
- a seducer
- a controller
- a liar
- an idol worshiper
- a promoter of illegitimate authority
- a very strong woman who married Ahab

In the New Testament (see Revelation 2:18–20) God refers to her as:

- a false prophetess
- a false teacher
- a seducer
- a fornicator
- an adulteress

Saints, God has stated that we are not to tolerate this type of seduction (see Revelation 2:20). Let us take a closer look at some of the characteristics of Jezebel so that we can more easily identify this seductive spirit and defeat it.

Jezebel Has No Gender

You might be wondering how Jezebel manifests in today's churches. Don't simply look for a strong, controlling, seductive woman. The Jezebel spirit has no gender. The spirit of Jezebel operates through male or female—anyone who allows it to control and use him/her will be the puppet of Jezebel.

Jezebel Labors with Ahab

In his book, _The Prophetic Fall of the Islamic Regime,_ Glenn Miller writes on the power of principalities. He exposes the structures of the demonic kingdom and the satanic hierarchies. He states, "Principalities work through personalities. Personalities influence people. And people destroy other people."[2]

This holds true for the Jezebel spirit. Every Jezebel has an Ahab, a personality she can influence, who labors with her in manipulation and control. Whether or not the spirit is married to an Ahab or has a ministry relationship with one, Jezebel finds someone to influence and manipulate to do her work. The Jezebel-Ahab team is at times an overpowering duo of such intimidation that many times senior leaders and entire congregations will bow their hearts to its threats and control.

Jezebel Desires Position

A Jezebel spirit desires to teach, especially before a proven time of trustworthiness. This spirit always pushes

191

ahead and intimidates leaders to gain her position. The spirit also is attracted to the prophetic ministry. Attempting to control intercession, the spirit will prophesy false visions and words to control intercession and prayer, thus releasing witchcraft prayers upon others.

The spirit always seduces others into her control by using false flattery. The spirit will say things like:

- "You can prophesy better than she can. You should be the prophetess of the house."
- "You are a more anointed intercessor than he is. You should be the head intercessor."
- "You are a much better teacher than she is. You are so much more anointed and gifted."

 These flattering words appeal to pride and are an attempt to gain a following. Their purpose is to draw in and seduce others in order to gain illegitimate power and authority.

Jezebel Desires Control

 Jezebel desires power and position because she wants total control. She will not remain in a place (or relationship) that she cannot control or manipulate.

Her name is translated "without cohabitation," meaning that she will not submit to or cohabitate with anyone. This further implies that she will not dwell with (work alongside) anyone she cannot control or manipulate, and she works against unity in any form. Jezebel is totally self-centered and self-serving.

 Jezebel attracts people with "soulish" connections—what I refer to as ungodly "soul ties." These are relationships of extreme codependency, an unnatural "needing" of one another and an emotional dependence. The spirit "binds" a person to itself so tightly that he or she feels bound in loyalty; in fact, the person feels that he or she will never be free.

I noticed that when I would battle against Jezebel, I would be exhausted most of the time. This is because of all the soulish prayers that were prayed—forms of charismatic witchcraft based on her selfish desires. Remember that witchcraft is a form of control, which is one of the main manifestations of Jezebel.

"I Am Not a Jezebel!"

I used to have many dreams about a false prophet. In the dream the false voice prophesied over my life. I would awake, rebuke any curses from the enemy and go back to sleep. One day I received the revelation of the dream. The Lord said that the false prophet in my dream was a stronghold of Jezebel. I argued with the Lord immediately, reminding Him, "I am not a Jezebel!" (Well, wouldn't you argue with God about that?)

Then finally I stopped defending myself and examined my heart. A soft voice spoke: *Sandie, what about idolatry? You have tried to maintain control all your life. You have desired your own will at times. This opened the door to idolatry, and Jezebel was an idolater.*

My mouth must have dropped to the floor. Talk about fast repentance! I knew the areas He was correcting. *Father, forgive me. I repent of all control. Empower me to utterly destroy all.*

Summarizing Jezebel:

1. Controls through flattery
2. Attempts to manipulate and control through false prophecy

3. Attracts the weak and codependent
4. Operates in confusion
5. Manipulates to get his or her way
6. Seeks position and power
7. Dislikes repentance
8. Promotes idolatry
9. Is attracted to false government
10. Dislikes authority
11. Stirs up strife and division
12. Operates in an atmosphere of frustration, fear and intimidation

It Takes a Jehu to Defeat Jezebel

 It took a Jehu (see 2 Kings 9) to destroy Jezebel. King Jehu was a commander who was anointed by God to conquer the Amalekites and Jezebel. Elisha sent a young prophet to Jehu, son of Jehoshaphat, son of Nimshi, to anoint him with oil as king of Israel. The prophet gave Jehu the following words:

> And thou shalt smite the house of Ahab thy master, that I may avenge the blood of my servants the prophets, and the blood of all the servants of the LORD, at the hand of Jezebel. For the whole house of Ahab shall perish: and I will cut off from Ahab him that pisseth against the wall, and him that is shut up and left in Israel: and I will make the house of Ahab like the house of Jeroboam the son of Nebat, and like the house of Baasha the son of Ahijah: and the dogs shall eat Jezebel in the portion of Jezreel, and there shall be none to bury her.
>
> 2 Kings 9:7–10

Jehu did not waste any time. He immediately killed Joram, the son of Ahab and Jezebel who was then king of Israel (Ahab had already died), and then Jezebel herself (see 2 Kings 9:27–37). After that Jehu had the other seventy sons of Ahab killed. Then "Jehu killed all who remained of the house of Ahab in Jezreel, and all his great men and his acquaintances and his priests, until he left him without a survivor" (2 Kings 10:11, NASB). He met relatives of King Ahaziah of Judah on the road who were coming to visit the royal princes and the sons of the queen mother, and he slaughtered all 42 of them (see verses 13–14). He went to Samaria and "killed all who remained to Ahab in Samaria, until he had destroyed him, according to the word of the LORD which He spoke to Elijah" (verse 17, NASB). Then Jehu assembled all the people and said to them, "Ahab offered Baal small service; but Jehu will offer much more." He summoned all the prophets of Baal, all his worshipers and all his priests. He told them to "sanctify a solemn assembly for Baal." All the worshipers of Baal came and entered the temple of Baal until it was filled from wall to wall. Then Jehu entered the temple and said to the worshipers of Baal, "Search and see that there is no worshiper of the LORD here among you, but only worshipers of Baal." Then they proceeded to offer sacrifices and burnt offerings. Jehu went outside to where his eighty guards were waiting and said to them, "Come in and kill them; let no one escape." They destroyed the temple of Baal and made it a latrine. Thus Jehu wiped out Baal from Israel (see verses 18–28). Up to that point in his life, Jehu utterly destroyed all, beginning with the wicked Jezebel, according to the word of the Lord.

It takes a Jehu to defeat Jezebel. It is important for us to recognize the characteristics of Jehu, so that we, too, can be empowered to rise up like he did and destroy our enemy:

1. Jehu was a commander. Like him, we must command the demonic stronghold to go.
2. He was a conqueror. We must conquer Jezebel with repentance and with the spirit of Jehu.

3. He was anointed. We must endure the processes of God in order to increase our anointing.
4. Jehu was determined to achieve his destiny. We must be like Christ and set our faces like flint toward our destinies.
5. He had a calling to smite his enemy, and he utterly destroyed all! Second Kings 9:7 says that God called Jehu to smite the house of Ahab. Whereas Saul had failed to smite the Amalekites, Jehu fulfilled the commission.
6. He slew the false prophets, tore down the false idols and halted false prophecy. Similarly, we must renew our minds and tear down all exalted imaginations.
7. Jehu used "full strength" against his enemy: "Jehu drew a bow with his full strength, and smote Jehoram" (2 Kings 9:24). We must also use full strength.
8. Jehu pursued his enemies. *Pursue* means that he followed in order to overtake and continued in order to accomplish (see 2 Kings 9:27). Just like King David, when he realized that his destiny was to pursue his enemy (the Amalekites), he was empowered to overtake and recover all. We, too, must pursue our enemy!

Defeating Jezebel

Dear ones, we are well able to slay the giant of Jezebel, which tries to abort our destiny! As I have stated before, repentance always brings breakthrough. I had to repent of opening the doors to Jezebel in my own life when God revealed those doors to me. If you have opened any doors and allowed any entrance to Jezebel, then I encourage you also to repent.

Let us consider the ways to defeat Jezebel:

1. Repent! (God's Word says that Jezebel never repented. She does not want you to repent either.)

2. Immediately separate yourself from this spirit/ person.
3. Remain submitted to delegated godly authority.
4. Remain teachable and accountable to authority.
5. Replace all fear with great faith.
6. Become a prayer warrior and be spiritually alert.
7. Develop and rely on your spiritual gift of discernment.
8. Remove yourself from all idolatry.
9. Seek servanthood over positions and titles.
10. Do not seek out an Ahab.
11. Develop a spirit of Jehu.
12. Continue to use your spiritual authority, using the keys of the Kingdom to bind the power of the enemy. Remember that you are seated in a place of authority with Christ Jesus (see Ephesians 2:6).

Again, the Lord is quite clear that we are not to tolerate the Jezebel spirit in our lives, our families, our churches, our cities or our nations. We must become like Jehu, rise up against the seductive Jezebel and utterly destroy all.

12
Twelve

Destroying the Seeds of the Generations
The Spirit of Athaliah

The LORD is longsuffering, and of great mercy, forgiving iniquity and transgression, and by no means clearing the guilty, visiting the iniquity of the fathers upon the children unto the third and fourth generation.

Numbers 14:18

The word *generation* means offspring, a period of time or a group of individuals belonging to a specific category. It is also referred to as a "life cycle."[1] A *cycle* relates to a recurring series of events or a repetition.

God has promised each of us complete deliverance from the sins of our previous generations. These mind-sets and strongholds are passed from one generation to another and hinder spiritual growth. He also has given us His word that our current and future generations will be protected. In order to be delivered from past generational sins and protect what lies before us—that is, in order to pursue destiny—we must destroy the negative spiritual strongholds that have influenced our generations.

One big generational stronghold from which we need to break free is the spirit of Jezebel. Her characteristics—control, manipulation, idolatry, etc.—have repeated themselves from one generation to another, and the Lord is exhorting us to break agreements we have made with the spirit of Jezebel and any behaviors influenced by it.

Praying against the Jezebel spirit is most definitely needed to halt planned seductions from our enemy, but we must not stop there. To ensure total victory over spiritual seduction, we must consider her generational seed in order to utterly destroy all. This means that we will have to destroy the generations of Jezebel.

Athaliah: "Whom God Afflicts"

Jezebel had a daughter named Athaliah who was twice as vicious and determined to destroy the anointed of God as Jezebel was. Being an offspring of both Ahab and Jezebel resulted in a double demonic influence. The spirit of Athaliah still operates today and must be destroyed.

Some theologians believe that Athaliah was the actual daughter of Jezebel and Ahab. Others believe that Omri was her father and that Ahab was her brother who later took her and functioned as her father. Some refer to her as Omri's granddaughter (see 2 Kings 8:18, 26). The word *daughter* in 2 Kings 8:26 is from the Hebrew translation: "a daughter in the wide sense and in terms of relationships, a branch, or company."[2] Whether she was a daughter or a granddaughter or not, we see the full revelation of this translation representing a "spiritual daughter" or "one of the same character and spirit" of Jezebel in operation. Using the term *branch* for the translation of *daughter* implies she was a branch or an offshoot from the "root" of Jezebel and Ahab.

The name *Athaliah* means "whom Jehovah has afflicted"— that is, with misery, pain, sickness or calamity.[3] Many times in Scripture afflictions were caused by curses upon the generations due to the sins of the ancestors. Since Athaliah was a descendant of Jezebel, a curse of affliction came upon her. She in turn inflicted pain and calamity upon others. Her name is derived from a root word that implies "to handle violently." She was aptly named, as she pursued violent acts of destruction to destroy the seeds of destiny in the generations. The spirit of Athaliah operates today with the same motive.

Athaliah was also the wife of King Jehoram of Judah and Judah's only queen who ruled from 841–835 B.C. (see 2 Kings 11; 2 Chronicles 22, 23). Her husband had the same character and spirit of Ahab. The daughter of Ahab and Jezebel, therefore, married and came into agreement with a man with an Ahab spirit.

Considering all that, the planned strategies of the thief become clearer. Let's examine the history of Athaliah more closely:

1. The daughter of Jezebel and Ahab had the same spirit as her parents.
2. She married a king who had the same spirit as her father, Ahab.
3. She inherited, through her bloodline, a hatred for true authority.
4. She inherited idolatry through her bloodline.
5. She inherited, through the bloodline of her mother, Jezebel, a determination to gain authority at any cost!

Athaliah, like her mother, worshiped the Canaanite god, Baal, and encouraged her husband to do the same.[4]

Evidently she had the ability to greatly influence and manipulate her husband, just as her mother controlled and influenced Ahab. Jezebel was the one who brought the false prophets and the idol worship of Baal into Israel. Now her daughter committed the identical act in Judah. *Judah* translates as "praise." Athaliah's intent was to destroy the praise of Jehovah and counterfeit the worship by praising the false god, Baal. Even today the Jezebel spirit attacks the pure praise and worship of God by attempting to seduce worship leaders and members of worship teams into sin and apostasy.

With her sights set on gaining more authority, she seized the throne of Judah upon the deaths of her husband and son. Her son died from battle wounds, and she immediately began her reign of terror in Judah. She murdered all her son's (Ahaziah's) male children because they were heirs to the throne (see 2 Kings 11:1).

The demonically inspired plan to seize total control and power, regardless of the cost, was hatched by Athaliah and was twice as destructive as the reign of Jezebel. Similar to King Herod, who much later destroyed all the male children in hopes of killing baby Jesus, Athaliah destroyed anyone who threatened her throne of authority.

The only child in succession who was not murdered was Joash, her youngest grandson. Interestingly, Athaliah's daughter, Jehosheba, took Joash and hid him from her mother for a total of six years. The queen's own daughter fought for the rightful lineage to the throne and saved her nephew's life.

Athaliah ruled for six years and was finally slain before her seventh year of illegitimate authority in Judah. It was Jehoiada, the priest, who rose up and led a revolt against the queen of Judah. The crowning of the child, Joash, as the rightful heir brought about the death of Athaliah (see 2 Kings 11:5–20). As the child was crowned, the people of Judah rejoiced, blew trumpets and declared, "God save the King!" Athaliah cried out, "Treason! Treason!" (The spirit of Jezebel always falsely accuses others of acts that really it is committing.) The priest then commanded that Athaliah be slain.

Examining more closely the characteristics of Athaliah, we identify the following manifestations:

1. a murderous spirit
2. the thief in operation (she would steal, kill and destroy to have her way)
3. jealousy
4. fear and intimidation
5. bitterness
6. rebellion
7. anger
8. pride
9. violent aggression
10. self-centeredness
11. false religion (Antichrist spirit)
12. idolatry
13. manipulation
14. control
15. seducing spirit
16. falsely accuses
17. lies and deceit

Slaying the Spirit of Athaliah

Dear ones, it took a Jehu to destroy Jezebel. To destroy Athaliah, it took the priest. In order to slay Athaliah's seed today, we must have the anointing of the priesthood.

Each of us is called as a "priest of the Lord." We have been chosen to serve Him. We are descendants of a royal lineage, called to show forth the praises of God and to rule and reign with godly authority.

But ye are a chosen generation, a royal priesthood, an holy nation, a peculiar people; that ye should shew forth the praises of him who hath called you out of darkness into his marvellous light.

1 Peter 2:9

Let's look more closely at a few characteristics of the priesthood:

1. The priesthood is consecrated.
2. The priesthood is anointed.
3. The priesthood serves in the house of God.
4. The priesthood is dedicated and committed.
5. The priesthood is holy.
6. The priesthood is clothed with righteous garments.
7. The priesthood is to "utterly destroy all."

We can be assured of victory if we commit ourselves to purification and consecration. By utterly destroying all areas of defilement and committing to our destiny, we will overcome the seduction of the enemy. It is our season to take off the old garments and exchange our clothing for the righteous garments of Christ Jesus.

The Sure Mercies of David

"Incline your ear, and come unto me: hear, and your soul shall live; and I will make an everlasting covenant with you, even the sure mercies of David" (Isaiah 55:3).

The "sure mercies of David" are the promises made to David and his seed—or "lineage" of authority. God made a covenant promise with David that David's seed would rule upon the throne forever. No matter what happened, even if David's children backslid, God promised that David's children would have authority.

Each time I travel to different churches, I recognize the demonic assignments against the next generation. The children of ministers, in particular, are targeted by seducing spirits. Satan has planned strategies to destroy our seed and our children's seeds of destiny.

But take heart! The sure mercies of David are ours. God has promised us the same as He promised King David. It may appear that the devil has snatched our children from us. It may seem as if we do not have the authority needed to protect our children. But according to God's Word, our children have a seated position with Christ Jesus. Dear ones, because of God's covenant promise neither your destiny nor your seed's destiny will be aborted.

The Anointed Must Rise Up

We must not overlook the seed from Jezebel's generation. Jezebel and her seed, Athaliah, tried to stop godly authority from rising up. But God's anointed rose up to defeat them and pursue their destiny in Him. In the same way today, anointed saints are called to defeat these two spirits by destroying their demonic assignments and then by taking their rightful places in God's destiny.

Thirteen

Shifting into Destiny

The LORD spake unto Joshua the son of Nun . . . saying, Moses my servant is dead; now therefore arise, go over this Jordan. . . . Every place that the sole of your foot shall tread upon, that have I given unto you, as I said unto Moses.

Joshua 1:1–3

On the morning of my sixteenth birthday I awoke to the radio music alarm. My heart was full of expectation and hope. I had been dropping big hints to both parents that I desired a car for my birthday. I had been driving the family station wagon long enough. After all, I had an image to protect.

Was I getting my heart's desire today? Would I run from the house to the garage and see my dream car fully materialized? I could visualize in my mind's eye that shiny red Stingray in full Technicolor. My palms began to itch for the keys.

I rolled over to turn off the alarm—and there they were! The keys to something!

But my excitement abated pretty quickly. I noticed the keys were not shiny and new. Even the key chain had a worn appearance, like a hand-me-down. The shape of the keys reminded me of our 1943 tractor that I often drove to mow our seven acres during the summer months.

I thought about that old tractor. It had taken me a solid month to master shifting its gears. The transmission suffered as I laboriously tried to shift into higher speeds. How I despised driving that tractor with those awful gears! I expected that my new car would have no gears to shift but be a smooth automatic transmission.

I snatched up the keys and ran outside, still holding onto my hopes. In full speed, I burst through the back door . . . and then came to a screeching halt as I first glimpsed my birthday present. There it sat, lifeless and still—and old.

What is it? I thought to myself. My mind raced backward, and I remembered seeing this type of car in my parents' family album. I recalled that they had one similar to this when they first married—more than 25 years ago!

I stood breathless. I finally had my own vehicle. I could now go anywhere in my own car. But could I be sure it would get me where I wanted to go?

"Well, what do you think?" My dad stood next to me, proudly viewing what he clearly believed to be a rare jewel. "I bought it yesterday. You have no idea how long I searched to find you just the right vehicle. What do you think of the color? It is a new paint job!" Obviously my dad loved the car. I think it was probably the same one he owned when he was a teenager.

I searched for the right words for an acceptable reply. Talk about having to shift gears! My thoughts raced as I dealt with my emotions and disappointment. The car was blue and not red. It was old, rather than new. It was not what I had pictured or desired. I forced myself to smile and focus on the fact that I now had my own car, regardless of what it was. I determined to enjoy the vehicle because it still represented freedom and maturity.

That car became known as "the Blue Bomb" around my high school. The guys thought it was cool to own a 1951 Chevy. After all, it was a three-speed, refurbished, with whitewalls—all foreign words to me until then. But to me, it was clunky, blue and antique. I was into new, shiny and sophisticated! And worst of all, I did not do well with shifting those old gears. That ancient car would hang in neutral as I drove. The Blue Bomb caused me more frustration than I can put into words. But the main thing I remember is that I detested the shifting!

Eventually I began to master the gears, and when it would get stuck in neutral, I would determine to ride through it until I could get the transmission to shift properly. It took me a while to convince my dad that, though I only drove on country roads, there may come a day when those country roads might not truly "take me home."

My dream car came one year later. It was still blue, not red—but it was new!

Shifts Defined

I often think of my first car when I think about a shift in the Holy Spirit. Shifting gears in a vehicle indicates that the driver is changing direction or speed. A shift represents moving from one place to another—a changing of position or levels.

Typing gives us another picture of shifting. We often use the "Shift" key to change typing techniques. A shift represents change.

Remember that while God never changes, God loves change. He continually is growing us in His Spirit. And in order to grow and mature in Him, we must shift gears.

A shift in the Spirit, therefore, indicates that there is some type of change taking place in our spiritual lives.

When I attempted to shift gears in that old car, I often got stuck in neutral. This can happen to us in the Spirit. Sometimes when we attempt to shift gears in the Spirit, we get stuck in neutral. Sometimes our "gears" grind as we struggle with rebellion toward God's changes. These areas of challenge slow down progress in God.

The Church is in a season of many supernatural shifts—both individually and corporately as a Body. God is shifting us from the old into the new. We are being challenged to let go of old religious mind-sets and the slavery mentality of Egypt.

As He shifts us out of Egypt, we must enter the wilderness for a season. Then comes the time when we must shift from the wilderness mentality into Canaan—our Promised Land. The Promised Land is just what it proclaims—a land that is promised to us and a land of fulfilled promises. It is our place of destiny.

In order for us to pursue this promised place of fulfillment, we must make a shift to renew our minds. We must shift from doubt and unbelief into the place of great faith. It is a shift from death into resurrection. We are being shifted

- from old wine to new wine;
- from old wineskins to new wineskins;
- from religion into present truth; and
- from old things to new things.

The Crossing

The book of Joshua begins with the Lord telling Joshua that Moses is dead. Joshua knows that already, so why does God have to remind him? Is God trying to hurt Joshua with the remembrance of his mentor's death? Is God being cruel? No!

No longer were the Israelites wandering through the wilderness. It was now God's appointed time for them to move into the Promised Land. God was reminding Joshua that the old had passed away. He was challenging Joshua to embrace an entirely new way of understanding Him. God was about to do a new thing, and He needed Joshua to understand the new way. God was about to move differently and lead His children differently. Spiritual leadership was shifting into a new dimension, and Joshua needed to understand the shift from the old to the new.

Let's examine the first three verses of the book of Joshua to understand God's new direction:

> Now after the death of Moses the servant of the LORD it came to pass, that the LORD spake unto Joshua the son of Nun, Moses' minister, saying, Moses my servant is dead; now therefore arise, go over this Jordan, thou, and all this people, unto the land which I do give to them, even to the children of Israel. Every place that the sole of your foot shall tread upon, that have I given unto you, as I said unto Moses.
>
> Joshua 1:1–3

Notice that God gave three instructions for the new direction:

1. Rise up.
2. Go over.
3. Your feet shall tread.

God's instructions to Joshua paint a beautiful picture for us of how to move into our destiny—our promised place in God. As we face moving forward into that new place, each of us must experience three shifts. First we must rise up and shift into deciding that we want to cross over into

211

the Promised Land. Secondly, we must shift into the place where we cross over the Jordan River. And the third shift is taking possession of our territory after we cross.

Shift One: The Decision

This was the season for Joshua to rise up and lead others to rise up. We cannot move forward without first rising up. This means that we are to make the decision to rise up from the dead and desolate areas of our lives. We will no longer sit and wait, but rather advance forward.

Making a decision is very hard for some of us. We postpone decisions for fear of making the wrong one. When facing a shift in the Spirit, however, it is not simply a decision of crossing over into a new place; it is deciding if we want to experience our promise.

Most of us are aware of our promises from God. His promises can come in the midst of personal prophecy, through prophetic preaching and insight, during our intimate times with Him, through a dream or a vision, or directly from His Word.

Webster's Dictionary defines *promise* as a declaration that something either will or will not be done. This definition reminds me of God's promise that He will fulfill His part if we fulfill our part. As the old adage goes, a promise is a promise! That is how God views His Word. If He promises, He is able to fulfill and complete that promise.

If we keep His words and commandments and remain obedient, for example, we will eat the fat of the land (see Genesis 45:18). If we do not remain obedient and faithful to Him, however, we will not receive our promised inheritance. So God's promises are often conditional.

In order to receive His promises in our lives, there is a condition: We must first decide to rise up and move forward. We must first make a decision to cross over into our destiny. Many of us have been trying to focus on crossing over without first truly deciding that we want to cross over. We are attempting to move forward with determination without making the firm decision that we want to move forward. We have been trying to take our promised inheritance without fixing our faces like flint toward destiny.

When we decide to take our promise, He gives us supernatural empowerment to move forward. At that precise moment the shift takes firm root and comes forth into maturity. Once the decision is made, and we are firmly fixed on the promise, then the Lord empowers us to move and shift into destiny. But there can be no supernatural empowerment until decisions are made.

Imagine yourself driving on a freeway. You come to a "Y" on the interstate and cannot decide which way to turn. If you do not make a decision, you will end up going straight into a barricade or some other obstruction. You might waver back and forth, slowing down traffic, which also could cause an accident. You are in danger until you make a decision. And you cannot accelerate until you decide.

It is the same when making a spiritual decision to move forward. Neither empowerment nor acceleration will occur unless we make the decision to move forward. In fact, it is dangerous to try and remain in the middle of the road.

Most of us are confined to old patterns of behavior. We have mind-sets concerning areas of the Spirit. We only know church the way we have experienced church. We cling to familiar songs, hymns and sermons. Can you imagine what would have happened if Joshua had not been willing to shift into a new mind-set, if he had decided to stay in the place God had him? The Israelites would have continued to wander in the wilderness and would have missed their destiny—their Promised Land.

But like Joshua rising up to lead the Israelites into the Promised Land, and like Abraham when he left Ur to go to the land God had promised him, we must shift out of the old and proceed into new areas. We must decide to move forward from our places of confinement. We must leave what is comfortable and familiar to move into greater places of blessing.

What will you decide?

Shift Two: Cross Over

God's second instruction to Joshua was to go over the Jordan. Similarly, we must go forth into our calling in Christ. This involves another shift. We may experience some "grinding of the gears" as we decide to go forth. We may even get stuck in neutral for a while. But we must keep our eyes on the prize of the higher calling!

A short season ago I was faced with a tremendous challenge. I had the opportunity to quit the ministry and begin selling real estate, as I used to do. I was offered a financial increase with a very promising future. Since pastoring a church seemed overwhelming and demanding, I was faced with a decision that would affect my destiny. Though it would eventually be my destiny to be released from pastoring a local church and begin to travel as a prophetess, this was not yet the time.

Satan desired for me to commit spiritual fornication—when he offers us something out of God's timing to thwart our destiny in Christ. This new job opportunity was a temptation from the enemy to deter me from God's intended destiny for me. The temptation was to leave my post before God released me.

I pressed into God, seeking an answer. My flesh wanted to go back to the old and familiar. I had been successful working in the world. I had been comfortable in my previous position, salary and title. I was not sure I could cross over into a destiny involving future ministry. It appeared too difficult.

I related to Naomi in the book of Ruth. Naomi had lost her husband and her two sons. Suffering from desolation and lost hope, she encouraged her two daughters-in-law to go back to their families, for she had nothing to give them. Similarly, I felt as if I had nothing left to give God's children.

Here I was, standing before my Jordan, contemplating my future. Could I cross over this Jordan? Could I truly believe in His promises? Could I hold onto my destiny link? Was I willing to die to my own desires, to take up my cross and follow Him? Like Naomi, I felt desolate and dead. I felt I could go no farther.

But then I thought about Ruth. While one of Naomi's daughters-in-law chose to go back home, the other one, Ruth, clung to her destiny link. As a result of clinging to Naomi, Ruth came into great favor. She ultimately married Boaz, had a child and became a great-grandmother to King David and an ancestor in the lineage of the Savior of the world. She clung to her destiny and fulfilled it. Like Ruth, I knew I had to choose to cling to destiny!

Ultimately, of course, I chose to cling to destiny by choosing to stay in ministry where I knew God wanted me to be. But I had to "go a little farther" to get there.

When you feel dead and when you are the driest, God will tell you to go a little farther. In Matthew 26:39, Jesus gathers His disciples together in the Garden of Gethsemane, and then Jesus goes "a little farther" beyond them. Each of us eventually comes to a "Y" in our path of life. At that place, there is a road that we come to called "a little farther." At that place along our journey we make decisions concerning our destiny. I have been at this crossroad several times since my job decision, and each time I must become even more determined for destiny because I must follow the road sign that reads "a little farther."

Those who desire all that God has for them will have to go "a little farther" than others. Many stop short of full destiny. So many of us press through the wilderness and then come to a complete halt just short of crossing over the Jordan. All too often, God's children lose focus and vision and then blame their dryness on others.

Be careful during the crossing over period. You might get cold feet and decide to return to Egypt, as the Israelites sometimes wanted to do (see Numbers 11). The leeks and garlic of the past seem inviting when you are staring at the challenges of moving forward.

Getting cold feet is part of the challenge of crossing over. After all, the priesthood stood in the riverbed of the Jordan holding the Ark of the Covenant for a long time while all the Israelites crossed over (see Joshua 3). The waters flowing from Mt. Lebanon were icy cold, and the priests had to place their feet in that water. Though the waters stood upon end and the land eventually became dry to allow passage, there was a season of cold feet.

As a pastor, I often feel that I have been "standing in the Jordan" for years, and my feet get cold at times! Sometimes I want to run in the opposite direction of God's leading. My flesh screams, I get confused and I cannot see. Coming from a background of tremendous insecurity, I have had to fight spirits of rejection many times. The Amalekite spirit continuously has robbed me of many Aarons and Hurs. At times I have been confronted with false accusations, which opened old wounds of abandonment and rejection. I have gotten cold feet so many times that I wanted to invest in a stock of electric blankets and socks! But like the priests in the Jordan—and like Joshua leading the people—I continue to choose destiny and remain with my destiny links.

All of us, if we are following the Lord as priests, will be tempted to run as we experience cold feet. But if we can endure the process of crossing over, then we will be richly rewarded. Remember, any pain is a down payment for future gain.

During these seasons of "cold feet" you will feel very alone, naked and vulnerable. During these tough times, Satan will tempt you to let go of your destiny links. Do not allow the enemy to convince you that you are to separate yourself from like believers or from spiritual authority. Be on guard! Do not pull away! Just as Ruth chose to remain close to Naomi—her destiny link—you must choose to stay closely connected to your destiny link. Some destiny links are relationships that God uses to connect us with His future purposes and plans. That pastor, leader, ministry or church may be the link to your destiny in God. It may be the teacher, mentor or situation that God can use to mature and empower you to move forward into your future.

God has given me several Naomis in my life—people who are my destiny links, to whom I must cling in order to walk into God's future plans for me. My spiritual father is Bishop Bill Hamon, the founder of Christian International. I know that the Lord placed me under his spiritual oversight so that I would be spiritually covered and grow spiritually. Being linked with Bishop Hamon links me with many others at Christian International. My husband also is one of my destiny links. I need all my destiny links to achieve God's full plan for my life.

Both my husband and I need destiny links. The ministers we oversee also need destiny links. Members of every congregation need destiny links with those in spiritual oversight.

Think of a chain and its links. The links of a chain link together and form one continual chain of links. If one link of chain gets disconnected, then the whole chain is broken. No longer is there oneness—a unity or flow of connected links. When there is a spirit of disunity at work in the spiritual realm, there is a disconnecting of the destiny links. The plan of the enemy is always to disconnect us from our destiny links.

God is very serious about unity. The Scripture says that unity brings life.

> Behold, how good and how pleasant it is for brethren to dwell together in unity! It is like the precious ointment upon the head, that ran down upon the beard, even Aaron's beard: that went down to the skirts of his garments; as the dew of Hermon, and as the dew that descended upon the mountains of Zion: for there the LORD commanded the blessing, even life for evermore.
>
> Psalm 133:1–3

The anointing is imparted from the head down. When we become disconnected from authority, the oil of anointing ceases to flow down upon us, breaking the links of our destiny chain.

When we cross over the Jordan, we must cross over in oneness. If we remain in unity, then we will move forward with much greater power and authority.

So to cross over into our Promised Land we must go a little farther. We must cross over fully, all the while holding fast to those in our lives whom God has given us as our destiny links. We must not blame our dryness on others or get cold feet. We must cross over in unity. And we must not allow the destiny thieves to steal our future. These are the shifts required for us to go forth over our Jordan, to move into our calling, our destiny in Christ.

Those who become determined will cross over fully. And it will be worth it, because at that time we shift into the blessing God has for us.

Shift Three: Taking Possession of Our Land

After crossing over into this new place, we are to begin to possess every place upon which our feet tread. To *tread* means to trample and march upon, signifying a military march and possession. It means that we are to make our mark upon the land, to stake our claim and drive our stakes into the ground, laying claim to our inheritance. Just as a miner finds gold and stakes his claim, we are to cross over, knowing that the gold has been laid up for us, and then stake our claim to our ground.

The word *tread* also implies making a great sound or a "sound of treading." In other words, as we move forward as an army we will make a great sound. Have you watched war movies and heard the sound a marching army can produce? It is powerful! To the enemy it is a threatening, terrorizing, dreaded sound.

I am reminded of the four lepers who went into the camp of their enemy, and the Lord magnified the sound of their feet. The enemy thought it was the sound of a marching army and began to flee. The three lepers took the spoils and then saved an entire city from starvation (see 2 Kings 7). The sound of treading is fierce and tormenting to our enemy!

The Lord was telling Joshua that as they took claim of their land, He would cause their footsteps to make such a great sound that it would cause the enemy to flee before them. Similarly, He calls us to tread upon the ground He is giving us, and our enemy will flee before us when he hears the sound of our feet on the Promised Land.

Know for a fact that giants inhabit the land God has promised you. Just as Israel faced all the -ites, you will face your own.

In order to engage those giants, we must learn to fight our battles from a place of victory. By this, I mean that we fight from the victory of our promise. First Timothy 1:18 states that we are to war a good warfare over each of our promises (prophecies): "This charge I commit unto thee, son Timothy, according to the prophecies which went before on thee, that thou by them mightest war a good warfare."

God has promised each of us a victory, and as mighty soldiers we wage warfare with that promise. Every promise becomes our sword of faith against the enemies that stand in our land.

If you are ever tempted to go back to Egypt, or return to old ways of thinking or responding, remember the direction the Lord gave the children of Israel:

> Only take heed to thyself, and keep thy soul diligently, lest thou forget the things which thine eyes have seen, and lest they depart from thy heart all the days of thy life: but teach them thy sons, and thy sons' sons.
>
> Deuteronomy 4:9

We must always take heed and never forget what God has done for us. It is a truth and a testimony that we are to pass on from generation to generation. We must pray over our promises, proclaim our victories and wage warfare in the Spirit. Doing these things will enable us to win our battle, to have our breakthrough, to take our Promised Land and to proclaim a powerful testimony of God's faithfulness.

We Need a Joshua

In order to possess the promise, we need a Joshua and not a Moses leading us. Most children of God do not realize this fact.

Though Moses was a very powerful leader, he was not the one God used to possess the land. Too many times, Moses interceded for the people to save them from God's correction. Moses eventually allowed the people to wear him down to the point where he gave in to the demands and whimpers of the people. This is why he could not cross over into his own promise.

God had to raise up another leader, Joshua, who knew how to fight for the promise. God had to shift the people from a preparation mentality to a possession mentality, and He needed a Joshua to lead them into this shift.

Though our flesh would like to hang onto a Moses, we all need a Joshua. We need the new wine that the leadership of Joshua represents. What is this new wine? It is a new way, a new direction.

Moses interceded at times when perhaps he should have allowed God to discipline. Moses is similar to many pastors today. All too often they allow their sheep to remain dependent upon them. They counsel by the hour and are there for the sheep upon demand. Many pastors are allowing codependent relationships with their flocks.

But there comes a time when sheep do not need intensive care, a time when sheep find the will of God for their lives and begin to mature. At this point, when the Lord wants to discipline His sheep, pastors must not intercede. The children of God will never be able to cross over and take the Promised Land if pastors do not allow them to fight for themselves. Pastors must choose to be Joshuas, leaders who will rise up to lead God's children into the battle for their inheritance.

Possessing the Promise

This does not mean you have to leave your present church to receive the new wine. Many times our present leadership is trying to bring in a new move, but we will not receive it. When we go through dry seasons we blame "Moses" rather than asking God why we are so dry. So many times we murmur and complain about our leaders, the programs, the way tithes and offerings are received. All too often we hold onto fears of authority, fears of failure and lack of faith. It is too easy to blame others for our personal lack of intimacy with God. We want to be like the Israelites. We want to be "saved" from our enemies rather than to rise up and possess our enemies. It is easier to blame Moses than to move forward with Joshua, who represents change.

Moses interceded for the people; Joshua represented what I refer to as the "Do It Yourself" ministry. In other words, rather than calling someone else to do the work for us, we must learn to pray ourselves, anoint ourselves and ask God ourselves. It is time to stop being too lazy to hear from God for ourselves. It is time to stop being so quick to blame others for their lack of discipline and breakthrough.

It is time for the Church to shift from immaturity to maturity. It is time for the Church to grow up so we can "go up" to a new level of God's glory. It is time to stop being like Moses in asking God to "show us Your glory." It is time to allow God to move us so that we will see His glory. It is time to allow Him to shift us.

In the wilderness, the Israelites followed the cloud by day and the fire by night. So many times I catch myself daydreaming of how easy that would be. As a pastor, I would not have to spend time in prayer seeking direction. I would simply get out of bed each morning, throw open the door and look for the cloud. I could easily know the direction of the Lord with my natural eyes.

Unfortunately, in the shift from Moses to Joshua, the cloud and fire ceased. The Israelites could move no longer by what they saw in the natural—no more clouds, fire, thunder or lightning. Instead they had to begin to move forward according to the word of the Lord. Since the directions were now coming from God to Joshua, then from Joshua to the congregation, the people had to gain a new level of trust in their new leader. They had to choose to hear the direction from Joshua. They had to experience a divine shift from seeing in the natural to seeing by the Spirit. The entire nation began to move into the promises based upon hearing the Word of the Lord and "seeing" breakthroughs by the Spirit.

We are in the same place as Israel as the people crossed over. As we mature, He is shifting us from the old cloud mentality into a faith mentality. We often cannot visualize the promise, but rather we must move forward with eyes of faith. God has given each of us a promise, a word concerning our destiny, and in faith we must begin to tread through our Promised Land. As we tread, we must believe in faith that God is going before us and defeating our enemies.

> Behold, I will make thee a new *sharp threshing instrument* having teeth: thou *shalt thresh the mountains*, and beat them small, and shalt make the hills as chaff.
>
> Isaiah 41:15 (emphasis mine)

In this passage the term "sharp instrument" actually means making a decision and being determined. In other words, our sharpness depends upon our determination. We cannot become a sharp instrument until we make a decision to serve God and be His instruments. Only by being determined can we receive the supernatural empowerment to be sharp.

Isn't this an awesome thought? God is simply waiting on us to make the decision to rise up, like Joshua, and like Caleb, and take what He has promised.

Dear ones, it is time to take your mountain! Make a decision today that you will shift into your destiny. Become fixed and determined that you will cross over the Jordan that stands before you. Begin to exercise your faith. Speak to every mountain, and watch the Lord remove the obstacles that are before you. He is your Father, and He desires to release your heart's desire. He will reward you as you diligently seek Him. And as you do, you will begin to experience your mountains moving!

RISE UP!!!

R espond

I n

S incere

E xpressions

U ntil

P urpose and destiny are accomplished.

List below actions that you need to take to accomplish your destiny and purpose. What responses are needed?

Fourteen

Caleb's Inheritance

Now therefore give me this mountain, whereof the LORD spake in that day; for thou heardest in that day how the Anakims were there, and that the cities were great and fenced: if so be the LORD will be with me, then I shall be able to drive them out, as the LORD said.

Joshua 14:12 (emphasis mine)

Wouldn't it be awesome if each of God's children had the determination that Caleb possessed? Is it possible for us, like Caleb, to recognize the mountains that block our breakthroughs and confess that nothing is too difficult for the Lord—that He can remove this obstacle? In faith, can we also proclaim, "Now therefore give me this mountain"?

As I discussed in the introduction to this book, Caleb had a different spirit, and for this reason he was able to take his land.

225

> Because all those men which have seen my glory, and my miracles, which I did in Egypt and in the wilderness, and have tempted me now these ten times, and have not hearkened to my voice; surely they shall not see the land which I sware unto their fathers, neither shall any of them that provoked me see it: but my servant Caleb, because he had *another spirit* with him, and hath followed me fully, him will I bring into the land whereinto he went; and his seed shall possess it.
>
> Numbers 14:22–24 (emphasis mine)

The Lord honored Caleb because he followed Him fully. Because of Caleb's faith in God's promises, he became even more empowered to take his possession.

The other Israelites, except for Joshua, chose to believe the evil reports of the ten negative spies. They feared the giants in the land. They focused on the size of the enemy rather than the promises. They even brought back large grapes and the fruits of the land, but their mouths spilled negativity, which overruled all God's promises to them.

The above passage states that all Israel had seen God's glory and the signs and wonders God performed on their behalf, yet Israel chose not to heed God's voice. They chose defilement, the seduction of Egypt and the old things. They continuously provoked God with their doubt and unbelief. They were, therefore, forbidden to cross over the Jordan into their inheritance. They were not allowed to possess the promise.

The old generation, which included Moses, died in the wilderness. Only Caleb and Joshua crossed over into their place of possession, along with an entirely new generation. Joshua led the new army—an army that had a new belief system and a new wineskin—into the new land.

Taking Your Hebron

Caleb's inheritance was Hebron. The Hebrew translation for *Hebron* is "association, company and communion."

Possessing new land requires unity, holiness and accountability. In order to take our land of Hebron today, God requires an army that is in covenant with each other—taking Communion together as the Body of Christ in unity.

When the Body of Christ takes Communion together, we are in communion. Holy Communion is a representation of covenant relationships—there is a sense of unity and oneness. Once the Body of Christ can truly become one with the Lord and His purposes, then we can become one with each other. When the army is "one," then the battle is "won"!

The word *Hebron* is derived from another root word and is translated "spells and charms." This indicates witchcraft, sorcery and curses. As the Body of Christ moves into its rightful inheritance, we will confront the occult powers of darkness. We will face wickedness, witches, covens and territorial spirits head on.

But we need not fear: The Lord will go before us and slay our enemy. As we use the keys of the Kingdom, binding the enemy and loosing God's perfect will, we will experience full victory!

The land of Hebron represents a promise for those who have the same spirit that Caleb exhibited. The same empowerment can be ours if we become determined for destiny.

The Grasshopper Mentality

Everyone has experienced fear. Children often fear the dark. Parents fear problems they may experience with their children. Businessmen fear failure and financial loss. CEOs fear losing power or organizations. Pastors fear losing their congregations. The saints of God fear authority or spiritual abuse. Everyone experiences fear at some time in his or her life.

The children of Israel experienced fear of the giants, who were descendants of Anak, a giant. Because they chose to focus on the giants rather than God's promise, they saw themselves as grasshoppers: "There we saw the giants, the sons of Anak, which come of the giants: and we were in our own sight as grasshoppers, and so we were in their sight" (Numbers 13:33).

Notice the verse does not say that the giants saw them as grasshoppers. Rather, the Israelites saw themselves as grasshoppers. The Israelites became intimidated due to the size of the giants.

So many times we focus on our limitations rather than choosing to believe what God says about us. God says we are not weak but strong. God says that we are chosen and blessed rather than insignificant. God says that we *can*, when we confess we *cannot*.

The Israelites had murmured and complained for so long that their hearts were consumed with negativity. They had sown into negative soil and could not begin to reap any positive fruit. If they had changed their "stinking thinking," then maybe a positive report could have surfaced.

Notice the characteristics of a grasshopper complex that are roadblocks to possession:

1. a doubting heart, negative speech
2. unbelief
3. distorted self-image
4. inferiority
5. lack of proper focus

It is important for us to begin now believing the reports of the Lord. Let's begin to sow our words properly, believing that what God has said will come to pass.

God can do anything! He can heal your self-image if you will commit to renewing your mind. Spend quality time in His Word and believe His promises. Faith comes by hearing God's Word. Spend time reviewing every personal prophecy you have received. Document the spiritual dreams and promises God has given. Begin to confess the Word of God over your life, your children, your home, your finances and your business. Renew your mind in these ways, and you will possess your Hebron.

To take your Hebron, you must:

1. Examine what you are speaking. Out of the abundance of the heart, your mouth will speak.
2. Wholly and completely follow the Lord.
3. Have faith in God's promises.
4. Keep your eyes on God and not on your mountain.
5. Be strong and have courage.
6. Remember: Once you decide on destiny, empowerment is released to fulfill destiny.

Get rid of the grasshopper mentality. Remain focused on destiny, and you will take your Hebron, as Caleb was empowered to do!

God Knows the Plans He Has for Us

You are never too old. It is never too late. You are well able to take your land! "'For I know the plans I have for you,' says the LORD. 'They are plans for good and not for disaster, to give you a future and a hope'" (Jeremiah 29:11, NLT).

Saints, we can do what He says we can do! We are empowered by His Spirit to take our land. Hebron is ours, and just like Caleb, we can become empowered to take our promised mountain.

Do not allow the destiny thieves to steal your destiny! Decide now to step forward and cross your Jordan into your Promised Land.

Begin now to take your Mountain! Go for it!

Notes

Introduction: I Want to Live and Fulfill Destiny!

1. *Webster's American Family Dictionary*, 1ˢᵗ ed., s.v. "destiny."

2. James Strong, *The New Strong's Exhaustive Concordance of the Bible* (Nashville, Tenn.: Thomas Nelson Publishers, 1984), ref. nos. 8615 and 6960.

3. *Webster's American Family Dictionary*, s.v. "determined."

4. Ibid., s.v. "thief."

5. Ibid., s.v. "steal."

6. Ibid., s.v. "secret."

7. Ibid., s.v. "exposure."

8. Ibid., s.v. "seduction."

Chapter 2: Overcoming the "Perilous Times"

1. *Enhanced Strong's Lexicon* (Oak Harbor, Wash.: Logos Research Systems, Inc., 1995).

2. For more information concerning prophetic training and learning to discern the voice of God, contact Zion Ministries at www.zionministries.us (817-589-8811) or Christian International Ministries in Santa Rosa Beach, Florida: www.christianinternational.org.

3. *Enhanced Strong's Lexicon.*

4. *Dream On* can be ordered by calling 817-589-8811 through Zion Ministries or by going to the website www.zionministries.us. Click on the product page; there are tapes available also.

Chapter 3: Belial

1. *Strong's Exhaustive Concordance*, ref. no. 1100.

2. Ibid.

3. *Regaining Vision* can be ordered from the website www.zionministries.us.

4. *Strong's Exhaustive Concordance*, ref. nos. 3290 and 6117.

Chapter 4: Purge Out the Leaven!

1. Ibid., ref. no. 692.

Chapter 5: The Seducing Amalekite Spirit

1. Ibid., ref. no. 5221.

Chapter 6: Aaron and Hur, Where Are You?

1. Ibid., ref. no. 7497.
2. Ibid., ref. no. 6003.
3. Ibid., ref. no. 2999.
4. Ibid., ref. no. 4569.
5. Ibid., ref. no. 3972.
6. Ibid., ref. no. 4613.
7. Ibid., ref. no. 4074.

Chapter 10: The Seduction of the Unclean Spirit

1. *Webster's American Family Dictionary*, s.v. "unclean."
2. *Strong's Exhaustive Concordance*, ref. no. 1294.

Chapter 11: The Jezebel Spirit

1. Bill Hamon, *Prophets, Pitfalls and Principles* (Shippensburg, Penn.: Destiny Image, 1991).

2. Glenn Miller, *The Prophetic Fall of the Islamic Regime* (Lake Mary, Fla.: Creation House Press, 2004), 69–70.

Chapter 12: Detroying the Seeds of the Generations

1. *Webster's American Family Dictionary*, s.v. "generation."
2. *Strong's Exhaustive Concordance*, ref. no. 1323.
3. Dr. Judson Cornwall and Dr. Stelman Smith, *The Exhaustive Dictionary of Bible Names* (North Brunswick, N.J.: Bridge-Logos Publishers, 1984), s.v. "Athaliah."
4. Walter A. Elwell, *Baker Encyclopedia of the Bible*, vol. 2 (Grand Rapids, Mich.: Baker Books, 1997), 229.

Recommended Reading

Davis, Dr. Jim. *Redefining the Role of Women in the Church.* Santa Rosa Beach, Fla.: Christian International Ministries, 1997.

Freed, Mickey. *Regaining Vision.* Bedford, Texas: Zion Ministries, 2002.

Hamon, Dr. Bill. *Prophets and Personal Prophecy.* Shippensburg, Penn.: Destiny Image, 1987.

———. *Prophets, Pitfalls and Principles.* Shippensburg, Penn.: Destiny Image, 1991.

———. *The Day of the Saints.* Shippensburg, Penn.: Destiny Image, 2002.

Hamon, Jane. *The Cyrus Decree.* Santa Rosa Beach, Fla.: Christian International Ministries, 2001.

Pierce, Chuck D. and Rebecca Wagner Sytsema. *The Best Is Yet Ahead.* Colorado Springs, Colo.: Wagner Publications, 2001.

———. *The Future War of the Church.* Ventura, Calif.: Renew Books, 2001.

Yoder, Barbara. *The Breaker Anointing.* Colorado Springs, Colo.: Wagner Publications, 2001.

 **Sandie Freed** travels nationally and internationally, speaking on dreams and visions, as well as delivering the prophetic word to church congregations and women's conferences. She teaches seminars on how to hear the voice of God and challenges believers to release their faith to receive prophetic impartations and flow in prophetic gifting. She is known for her powerful, down-to-earth messages that release life transformation and encouragement.

Sandie has a master's degree in biblical theology and has been a featured television and radio guest speaker on dreams and visions, eating disorders and deliverance. Sandie has authored *Dream On*, which not only discusses the importance of dreams and visions but also empowers every reader to interpret his or her own dreams.

For information on Zion Ministries' seminars, such as *The School of Prophets*, *Advanced Prophetic Training* and *Prophetic Intercession Training*, as well as recent teachings, books, tapes or itinerary, or to contact the author concerning speaking engagements, please contact:

Zion Ministries
P.O. Box 54874
Hurst, Texas 76054
(817) 589-8811
Email: zionministries1@sbcglobal.net
Website: www.ZionMinistries.us